Democratic Education in a Multicultural State

Edited by
Yael Tamir

**Blackwell Publishers/The Journal of the Philosophy of Education
Society of Great Britain**

Copyright © The Journal of the Philosophy of Education Society of Great Britain 1995

ISBN 0-631-19925-X

First published in 1995

Blackwell Publishers
108 Cowley Road, Oxford OX4 1JF, UK
and
238 Main Street, Cambridge, MA 02142, USA.

British Library Cataloguing in Publication Date
A CIP catalogue record for this book is available from the British Library

Library of Congress Cataloguing-in-Publication Data
Democratic Education in a Multicultural State / edited by
Yael Tamir
p. cm. — (Journal of Philosophy of Education Monograph series: 1)
Includes Index. ISBN 0-631-19925-X (alk. paper)

1. Multicultural education   2. Education — Philosophy.
3. Democracy — Study and teaching.
I. Tamir, Yael.   II. Series.
LC1099.D45 1995   370.19′6 — dc20   95-14114

Printed in Great Britain by Redwood Books, Trowbridge.
This book is printed on acid-free paper

Contents

Preface

The multicultural nature of most modern societies raises important questions about education. From the fairy-tales of the kindergarten to the history taught to older children and the literary 'canon' of the university, and not excluding topics in science and mathematics, almost any curriculum can be challenged on the grounds that it is partial and represents the outlook, and reinforces the power, of one cultural, racial or religious group, or of one sex, rather than another. And from time to time controversy erupts in particularly intensive form, as it has done in recent years over the teaching of evolution, for example, over whether *Huckleberry Finn* is a 'racist' text, and whether (a much publicised case involving a London primary school) *Romeo and Juliet* is educationally unsuitable in celebrating an exclusive heterosexuality.

One solution to these difficulties, which has commended itself to some in the UK at least, is to talk briskly of 'our' culture and heritage and their transmission. Thus 'English' rather than 'Language' as a school subject and the insistence that schools should reflect a predominantly Christian society; thus too the importance of the commemoration of the past, especially a wartime past when, it seems, the whole country pulled together as one. These are brave attempts to preserve unity from fragmentation, but they risk denying difference and diversity, and silencing voices which have another story to tell.

The liberalism which insisted that the state should be neutral between different substantive versions of how life should be lived has of course been regularly criticised over the last decade or so for offering insufficient moral or civic guidance. And many philosophical problems have been found in liberalism and the deontological ethics on which it is usually built, including the unsatisfactorily thin picture that emerges of persons as essentially lonely choosers, their identity fixed antecedently to their ends, commitments and associations. Hence some have preferred another version of liberalism under which the state promotes particular, substantive versions of culture while protecting basic rights. From here it is a short step to embracing communitarianism *as opposed to* liberalism, and perhaps to regarding education as a principal instrument in state-sponsored efforts to form a cohesive sense of national identity.

Communitarianism too has its different and competing versions. Community might be a matter of having certain sorts of feeling or fraternal sentiments. It might be a way of combining to pursue our individual projects and choices more effectively. Most interestingly, from an educational viewpoint, we might conceive our very identities as defined to a degree by the community or communities of which we are a part. Community would then describe 'a mode of self-understanding partly constitutive of the agent's identity'[1] in a way that

1

would have been familiar to John Dewey, for whom democracy is precisely 'the best means so far found . . . for realizing ends that lie in the wide domain of human relationships and the development of human personality'.[2]

Dewey, so often treated at present as a chief source of our educational problems, saw education as the laboratory of philosophy, and philosophy as 'the theory of education in its most general phases'.[3] This book, which is also the first Special Issue of the *Journal of Philosophy of Education*, provides a fine example of the peculiarly intimate connection between philosophy and education: our understanding of multiculturalism in our schools and universities and our understanding of the nature of a liberal, democratic state inform each other. The chapters below were for the most part given as papers at the International Conference on Education for Democracy in Jerusalem in 1993. The Philosophy of Education Society of Great Britain and the *Journal of Philosophy of Education* are grateful to Yael Tamir for editing this collection.

RICHARD SMITH

NOTES

1. Michael Sandel, *Liberalism and the Limits of Justice*, Cambridge University Press 1982, p. 150
2. Democracy and educational administration, *School and Society* 45.1162, 1937
3. *Democracy and Education*, Macmillan, 1916

Two Concepts of Multiculturalism

YAEL TAMIR

In the last two decades political reality has undergone such rapid changes that it is hard to remember that, not long ago, Fukuyama announced that we had reached the end of history. Liberal democracy, he argued, had been declared the winning party. It had managed to drive all its rivals off stage; all future debates would be no more than variations on a theme — the liberal theme.

It is now clear that such celebrations were premature and that, even though liberal democratic values and politics have gained considerable support in the last decades, their success was by no means conclusive. In fact more and more liberal democrats recognise the need to find ways of functioning within a multicultural setting. Multiculturalism, Raz argues, 'requires a political society to recognise the equal standing of all stable and viable communities existing in a society'.[1] While some of these viable and stable communities share liberal values and democratic convictions, others are authoritarian and illiberal. Does the ideal of multiculturalism apply equally to both types of communities? In order to answer this question we must distinguish between two very different concepts of multiculturalism. The first is a *thin* one which involves different liberal cultures; the second, *thick multiculturalism*, involves liberal as well as illiberal cultures. The former leads to a particular type of interest-group politics, the latter to a *modus vivendi* which is based on two, very different, points of view: a liberal one which emphasises respect for different ways of life, and an illiberal one which seeks to secure its own existence in the midst of a liberal society.

THIN MULTICULTURALISM

The debate between the English- and French-speaking communities in Canada is an example of thin multiculturalism. As the two communities share a set of liberal-democratic beliefs, the debate is an intra-liberal one. It involves two competing interpretations of liberalism which Walzer calls liberalism 1 and liberalism 2. Liberalism 1 is committed to individual rights and 'almost by deduction from this, to a rigorously neutral state'.[2] Liberalism 2, on the other hand, 'allows for a state to be committed to the survival and flourishing of a particular culture', as long as the basic rights of citizens are all protected.[3] These two types of liberalism are structured to meet the needs of individuals found in different actual circumstances: the former is more proper for immigrant societies wishing to promote cultural integration, the latter for members of states which are either culturally homogenous or composed of several distinct, territorially well-defined, cultural societies.

In cases of thin multiculturalism, problems of cultural relativism, a lack of common discourse or disagreements over basic principles do not arise. The debate over the future of Canada does not stem from French Canadians having difficulties in understanding the culture, language or traditions of English Canadians; there is no cultural barrier they cannot cross. In fact part of the problem is the similarities between the two cultures which allow for easy mobility and assimilation. The two groups thus understand each other perfectly well but have different interests, cultural interests. This kind of multiculturalism thus calls for a particular version of interest-group politics.

As in cases of interest-group politics the state is supposed to remain neutral between the different interest-groups, liberalism 1 rather than liberalism 2 seems to be the adequate solution for cases of thin multiculturalism. Indeed, according to Walzer liberalism 2 is an exception, which allows the provincial government of Quebec to deviate from liberalism 1 and act for the preservation of French culture. 'This is precisely to make an exception; the federal government would not itself take on this Quebecan project or any other of a similar sort. Vis-à-vis all the ethnicities and religions of Canada, it remains neutral; it defends, that is, a liberalism of the first kind.'[4] But surely the Quebec case is no exception at all. In fact the Quebecois desire to have liberalism 2 has come about because the Canadian government, despite its commitment to liberalism 1, has drifted towards liberalism 2; that is, it cannot remain genuinely neutral with regard to cultural issues. Consequently French Canadians feel excluded and marginalised within the greater Canadian system and want a political system they could see as their own.

In practice the difference between the two forms of liberalism is less profound than it may seem. In fact it is only because liberalism 1 is not a viable practical option that liberalism 2 emerges as an alternative. Yet as this alternative retains, in practice and in theory, a commitment to the ideal of individual rights embodied in liberalism 1 the close affinity between the two forms of liberalism is retained.

The difference between these two types of liberalism thus seems to lie in the awareness of the state that it cannot but promote some particular culture(s), a fact that is as easily noticed by members of minority groups as it is unnoticeable to members of the majority. Hence it could be claimed that both the Quebec and the Canadian government adopt liberalism 2. The Quebecois, however, perceive their culture to be actively threatened in a way that the English Canadians do not feel theirs to be; therefore, the Quebecois government is motivated to take more extreme and explicit measures for cultural protection than does the federal government. Were the culture of the English-speaking community rather than that of the French-speaking community found under threat, the cultural nature and policies of the Canadian rather than the Quebec government might have become more evident. This suggests that the difference between the two societies is not that Quebecois society devotes itself to a common good, and thus deviates from the model of the neutral state which the English society retains and fulfils to the letter. Rather, as the common good of the English-speaking community is well protected, one needs no special measures to protect it, and it is taken for granted. It has become a latent common good, and as long as it is not threatened it will not be consciously pursued.

As governments cannot be culturally neutral, all states, including all liberal states, are culturally biased, and may thus be either mono-cultural or multicultural. Very few are overwhelmingly mono-cultural; Portugal, Iceland, Norway or Japan might be examples. Most states, however, fall within the second category and differ only with regard to the degree of their internal diversity. They can be bi-cultural, including two cultural groups of almost equal size and economic power, as in the case of Belgium or the former Czechoslovakia. Some are divided between a large majority culture and one or more minority cultures, as happens in Britain, Israel or Spain. Finally, some are genuinely multicultural, including several cultural groups of fairly similar size, as in Switzerland, or (to mention a much less peaceful example) the former Yugoslavia. In each of the three types of states the different cultural groups have specific interests they strive to protect, the most common of these being the preservation and protection of their own cultural identity. These interest-based struggles will not fade away, even if all the relevant cultures share liberal beliefs and values, because members of each cultural group also entertain communal commitments and strive to carve a place for their own culture, history and language in the public sphere. Yet, despite the persistence of such struggles, an overlapping consensus could be achieved between the different liberal groups, as members of all these groups are likely to adopt some version of Rawls' two principles of justice, provided that cultural goods—in particular the ability to enjoy a rich and lively cultural environment—are added to the list of the primary goods.

The latter element is an important one as it calls for certain transformations in the structure of the political process. Conflicts over particular interests, whether individual or group ones, are commonly solved by allowing the different groups to participate in democratic decision-making processes. As long as individuals have an equal opportunity to present their views and participate in a fair process, the fact that their preferences might be outvoted is not regarded as unfair. Members of other groups — communists, vegetarians, opera lovers — may find themselves time and again in a minority position, unable to influence, let alone imprint, political institutions and culture with their own beliefs, preferences or norms of behaviour. Yet they could hardly claim that they have been treated unjustly or that their rights have been violated. Where the community is pluralistic and heterogeneous, the fact that one can be outvoted on a variety of issues is unavoidable.

Why is it, then, that the inability to protect cultural interests — even if that inability results from a fair political process — is seen as unfair? The first answer that comes to mind has to do with the fact that cultural interests are, by their very nature, restricted in their reach. That is, the interests are in most cases restricted to members of a particular group (though in some cases non-members may also have an interest in the protection of a certain culture). Hence such interests are unlikely to gain support in a fair democratic process. But this is true also of some of other groups, as opera lovers or vegetarians are also likely to remain a minority. The crux of the matter then is neither the size of the group, nor the fact that a certain interest is likely to be permanently outvoted, but the nature of that interest. Cultural interests are identity-bound interests, interests which relate to one's desire to preserve one's identity, and are therefore of particular importance. It is this special feature of the interests that makes them particularly worthy of respect.

Though the emergence of identity-bound interests developed only in the aftermath of the struggle for equal rights they become part and parcel of a liberal struggle for equal concern and respect. This development derives from the growing recognition that state neutrality is an ideal which cannot be achieved. In the early stages of their struggle for equal rights and integration, members of minority cultures endorsed the image of the state as culturally and normatively neutral. In their attempt to gain equality, members of these groups tended to reject any deviation from universalist arguments, fearing it would legitimise discrimination.[5] As is demonstrated by the history of Blacks in America, of Diaspora Jews, and of Sephardic Jews in Israel, disillusionment, strangely enough, came hand in hand with success, with the political empowerment of national and ethnic minorities.

Members of disempowered minorities soon discovered that being granted a set of formal civic rights was insufficient to ensure equal status, and realised that they had to decide which was the lesser of two evils: remaining estranged and marginalised, or integrating at the price of self-effacement. Members of such minorities thus became increasingly aware that the ideal of a culturally neutral public sphere embodies a dangerous and oppressive illusion.[6]

Yet, haunted by the shadows of 'separate but equal' policies originally meant to preserve segregation and social inequality in education, members of cultural minorities were reluctant to demand special schools or classes aimed at fostering their own tradition, language and history. They faced a dilemma: demanding such measures would imply not only an acknowledgement but also an acceptance of the particularised nature of the state; ignoring their need for particularised schools and communal institutions would considerably reduce their chances of retaining their identity. It was only when it became clear that no struggle for equal rights could turn the state into a culturally neutral institution that national minorities began to demand special treatment in the name of equality. Being granted equal rights, they realised, is not enough, as strict adherence to the principle of equal treatment tends to perpetuate oppression or disadvantage. The notion of universal citizenship had therefore to be replaced by one of 'differential citizenship'.

The public sphere in a multicultural state is thus supposed to be varied, to reflect the particularities of its members. Citizens are no longer expected to transcend their particular, self-interested lives in order to participate in public discussions and collective decision-making; yet they do need a shared basis of consensus in order to be able to agree on a set of basic political principles. In the case of thin multiculturalism, Rawls' overlapping consensus or Dworkin's abstract egalitarian principle seem well-suited to filling the need for guiding principles. Suppose the parties in the original position, who have general knowledge of their society's basic features, are aware of the fact that their state encompasses various national, ethnic and cultural groups, but do not know which of the particular groups they belong to. Under such conditions they are likely to endorse Gutmann's view that 'the dignity of free and equal beings requires liberal democratic institutions to be nonrepressive, nondiscriminatory, and deliberative'.[7] They are also likely to accept Young's demand for providing institutionalised means for the explicit recognition and representation of oppressed or disadvantaged groups.[8] Without such organising principles, granting representation to the different cultural groups might lead to further oppression, as stronger groups might abuse and oppress the weaker ones which would, in turn, use their power to exploit those weaker than themselves.

In her critique of interest-group politics, Young argues that such politics forestalls the emergence of public discussion and decision-making, as no group needs to consider the interests of others 'except strategically, as potential allies or adversaries in the pursuit of one's own. The rules of interest-group pluralism do not require justifying one's interest as right or as compatible with social justice.'[9] The contrary, she argues, is true for a heterogeneous public 'where participants discuss together the issue before them, and are supposed to come to a decision that they determine as just or most just'.[10] Young's criticism of interest-group politics, however, seems just as relevant to cases of ethnic and cultural group politics. The politics of difference is no more inherently correlated with a desire for justice than is interest-group politics.

It is puzzling to find that supporters of multiculturalism, who stress the importance of power relations, aim to revive the old liberal belief in social harmony inspired by an invisible hand. This belief is the unavoidable, and unrealistic, outcome of their rejection of liberal principles as the basis of political discussion and decision-making. If there are no general principles upon which members of the different cultural groups can agree, then idealised, invisible-hand solutions seem the only available fallback position. Ideally, Young claims,

> a rainbow coalition affirms the presence and supports the claims of each of the oppressed groups or political movements constituting it, and arrives at a political program not by voicing some 'principle of unity' that hides differences but rather by allowing each constituent to analyze economic and social issues from the perspective of its experience.[11]

But promoting an illusion of harmony within diversity is as dangerous and oppressive as the old liberal illusion of neutrality. It is only when this illusion is rejected that we are able to consider various models of conflict resolution, appreciate the advantage of the liberal democratic model and fashion the educational tools necessary for its construction and endurance.

The evident national, cultural and religious diversity of a society makes necessary a thin layer of civic education, introducing children to the liberal discourse of rights and rationality. Without that thin civic education, it will be impossible to generate cross-cultural discussions based on equal respect and concern for all participants.

In a multicultural political system, be it a town, a state, a federation, a regional organisation or a global society, it is especially important that all children learn to respect others who have different life styles, values and traditions and learn to view them — *qua* members of the political system — as equals. Beyond this thin layer each cultural group can foster among its youth knowledge which is relevant to their own particular community, its history, language and traditions. Civic education should therefore create civic friendship among all members of the political community; but it should attempt to do so, not by assimilating all members into one culture, but by respecting cultural diversity. All children should thus acquire some knowledge of the culture, history and tradition of all national groups that share their political system, and be taught to respect them.

Hence it is the strengthening of multiculturalism, and with it of demands for allowing particular cultural groups to deviate from the public school system, that highlights the importance of civic education, and it is a respect for and a belief in the importance of belonging to thick cultures that motivates the search for a thin layer of agreement.

Democratic education in a multicultural state thus seems to demand three layers of education: a unified stratum of civic education (which in fact will be similar in all multicultural societies), a particularistic stratum of communal education, and a shared stratum of cross-cultural education which will introduce children to the diversity of their own society. This threefold structure is assumed to meet the cultural needs of members of minority communities, while still attempting to preserve a somewhat fragile but nevertheless stable political union based on equal participation in a shared political process. All that democratic education demands, Walzer argues, is that all children be taught the history, the philosophy and the political practice of democracy. But this suggestion, as he acknowledges, is not as minimal as it might seem: democracy, especially liberal democracy, 'has a substantive character; it is not a neutral procedure but a way of life'. Democratic education could thus be seen, by cultures which foster illiberal and undemocratic values, as 'a program for cultural subordination', and they are thus likely to resent it.[12] Such resentment, which features in cases of thick multiculturalism where the debate is not an intra-liberal one but one between liberal and illiberal cultures, may make social agreement impossible.

THICK MULTICULTURALISM

We should then look at this second type of multiculturalism which raises far more difficult issues, as it calls for a compromise between a liberal and an illiberal point of view. Here questions of cultural relativism and the inability to converse across conflicting systems of belief may arise. Take for example the recent debate in France between supporters of French tradition, culture, and (especially) the traditional French understanding of the notion of citizenship, on the one hand, and Muslim citizens of France on the other. The debate concerns the right of girls and women to wear a *hidjab* in schools and universities. According to the French civic tradition these institutions are to be culturally and religiously neutral and hence before entering such public institutions individuals should shed all distinguishing features, be they a *hidjab*, a skull cap, a turban or whatever. These garments could, of course, be worn in the private sphere, which is the proper sphere in which to express particular identities. Hence the French education minister, François Bayrou, asked secondary school principals to ban 'ostentatious signs' of religion, a code phrase for headscarves. The French, says a government official, want Muslims to behave like them. 'If Muslims want to impose their costumes, wear veils, that generates a backlash. Muslims born in France who don't want to become French are fanatics or invaders.'[13] Our only ambition, replies Abdallah Ben Mansour, president of the Union of Islamic Organisations in France, 'is to become at the same time good Muslims and good French citizens. But as long as people wage campaigns on the peril of Islam, as long as we let rancours and frustrations accumulate, we will encounter all forms of radicalization.'[14] Hence what French officials see as imposing neutrality Muslims see as a campaign against Islam. This is not an incidental disagreement: it reflects the cultures of both groups, as the idea that religion or culture could remain strictly private is one that fits well a Western Christian society but is daunting to Muslims or Jews whose religion cannot be restricted to the private sphere. No orthodox religious Jew can agree to take off his skull cap at school, or in court, or in parliament — God's commands apply everywhere and could not be overridden by state law. Why should we change Islam, radical Muslims ask. 'The second a Muslim makes a reconciliation, he's disobeying Allah. Divine law goes ahead of any other law.'[15] If the law of God, or of the tribe, takes priority over state law, then the conflict seems to be unsolvable (unless the law of God, or the tribe's tradition, is a liberal democratic one). 'When a conflict involves systems of values so opposed that the adherents of each not only think the other completely wrong, but they cannot accord the others freedom to act on their values without betraying themselves',[16] it cannot be resolved by agreement on a set of governing principles or by achieving an overlapping consensus.[17]

Can a thick multicultural society find a way to counter cultural conflicts? This question cannot be ignored as most multicultural societies include illiberal as well as liberal cultures. The need to come to an agreement with such cultures motivates Rawls' attempt to draw guidelines for a Law of Peoples which will be acceptable to members of both liberal and illiberal communities. Rawls attempts to bridge the gap between liberal and illiberal cultures by introducing an intermediary notion of well-ordered hierarchical societies, or reasonable societies. These societies, though illiberal, follow four principles: (a) they are peaceful and gain their legitimate aims through diplomacy and trade; (b) their system of law is sincerely and not unreasonably seen as guided by a common good conception of justice; (c) their institutions include a reasonable consultation hierarchy; and (d) citizens are seen as responsible members who can recognise their moral duties and obligations and play a part in social life. Moreover, such societies admit a measure of liberty of conscience and freedom of thought, even if these freedoms are not in general equal for all members. For these reasons, Rawls argues, reasonable societies could agree to a Law of Peoples which is based on thin liberalism.[18]

Rawls' attempt might seem futile as most illiberal societies are not reasonable ones and are unlikely to agree to the Law of Peoples he offers unless forced to do so. Yet his attempt is important as it draws the limits of a possible compromise between liberal and illiberal cultures. Such a compromise becomes possible as a result of a distinction between two kinds of liberalism: *rights-based* and *autonomy-based* liberalism. The former takes the rights of individuals to be paramount without conceiving of those rights as grounded in autonomy-entitlement and choice prerogatives. Hence it can express not only toleration but also respect for decent illiberal cultures which do not foster the ideal of personal autonomy but which respect their members and allow them some means of participation and social influence. Autonomy-based liberalism, on the other hand, tolerates and respects only autonomy-supporting cultures — namely liberal ones. It thus cannot avoid the trivialisation of pluralism.

Many liberals may take personal autonomy to be paramount; they understand human dignity to consist largely in autonomy, that is 'in the ability of each person to determine for himself or herself a view of the good life'.[19] Membership of cultural, religious or national groups is thus seen as valuable only to the extent that it provides a context for choice, an evaluative horizon (to use Taylor's term). Espousing the ideal of an autonomous life, autonomy-based liberalism ranks communities by their potential contribution to the conditions of autonomy: namely by their contribution to their members' ability to develop 'appropriate mental abilities, a suitable range of options, and independence'.[20] Using this categorisation, autonomy-based liberalism judges illiberal cultures to be inferior to liberal ones.

As members of such cultures insist on 'bringing up their children in their own ways', Raz writes, they are, 'in the eyes of liberals like myself, harming them'. According to an autonomy-based liberalism liberals have a right, or perhaps even a duty, to promote the assimilation of illiberal cultures. Raz thus suggests that liberals are justified in taking action to assimilate minority cultures, including the destruction of separate schools, even at the cost of letting the culture die or at least be considerably changed by absorption and the break-up of the community.[21]

Yet assimilation is not the necessary conclusion of a rights-based liberalism, which places at its core a commitment to equal concern and respect for individuals, their preferences and interests, regardless of the way these were formed. In fact liberalism, in its more traditional form, was committed to protecting a set of freedoms which were meant to allow individuals to pursue their preferences, desires and interests, regardless of whether these were formed autonomously or were forced upon individuals by their culture or tradition. Developing a detailed distinction between autonomy-based and rights-based liberalism ranges beyond the scope of this paper, yet it is important to see the implication of this distinction for the issue of multiculturalism.

Since autonomy-based liberalism regards communities which do not foster autonomy as inferior to ones that do, it endorses toleration towards illiberal cultures only as a means for a slow, yet permanent, liberalisation of such cultures. Rights-based liberalism, on the other hand, is devoted to the protection of all cultures which provide their members with a decent environment and life chances. 'Given that even oppressive cultures can give people quite a lot, it follows that one should be particularly wary of organized campaigns of assimilation and discrimination against "inferior" and oppressive cultures. They provide many of their members with all that they can get.'[22] On this view respect for illiberal, reasonable communities which are valued by their members, even if they fail to provide (or even prevent) the chance to develop autonomous lives, is derived from respect for the right of individuals to live according to their values, traditions and preferences, as long as these do not involve harm to others. Hence for rights-based liberalism the question is not which cultures allow individuals to develop their autonomy in a better, more comprehensive way, but rather which societies individuals would like to live in.

As Mendus forcefully claims, autonomy-based liberalism prevents us from appreciating other cultures: 'as autonomy valuers we lack the moral language with which to provide an explanation of their humility as anything other than oppression'.[23] Hence we may fail to appreciate that 'there are virtues which are valuable, yet which cannot properly be accommodated within a moral framework which gives centrality to self-assessment and autonomy'.[24] Rights-based liberalism might be more open-minded about the set of values offered by different cultures and attempt to listen to their different voices. Moreover, rights-based liberalism might see multiculturalism as a way of enriching the liberal perspective and as a means for self-understanding. Feinberg sees multiculturalism in a similar light, as a policy of 'decentring and of coming to terms with otherness'. This, he argues, is the major task for the education of a democratic public in a multicultural society.[25]

Rights-based liberals might then respect other cultures and see multiculturalism as a valuable tool for learning about others as well as about themselves; yet for defenders of illiberal cultures such encounters are much less welcome. Illiberal groups, Wringe argues, see such reflective ventures not only as 'misguided and spiritually dangerous to their members but as threatening to their group's identity and even its continuous existence'.[26] Halstead supports this claim, bringing into the discussion the point of view of religious minorities. Such minorities, he argues, cannot accept an education in which 'for 95% of the time their children were subject to a neutral or a secular curriculum while 5% was devoted to their own cultural or religious beliefs and practices'.[27] This asymmetry is well expressed also in the Mozert case discussed by Macedo. In this case some fundamentalist and evangelical families demanded that their children be excused from participating in a reading programme which they claimed interfered with the free exercise of their religion by 'exposing the children to a variety of religious points of view in an even-handed manner, thus denigrating the truth of their particular religion'.[28] This asymmetry is reflected in the divergent attitudes held towards the idea of cross-cultural exchanges in Israel. While liberal Israelis, whether secular, Jews, Muslims or Christians, endorse the idea of multiculturalism out of respect for others, thus allowing all cultures to introduce their traditions and values in schools, as well as on public television or radio, and are constantly ready to make efforts to allow members of such cultures to retain their ways of life, their openmindedness is not reciprocated. Exposure to cultural exchanges is therefore not mutual; liberals expose their children to illiberal forms of life while defenders of illiberal cultures make a special effort to shelter their children from any form of cultural diversity. Taking into account that complete closure is impossible, members of illiberal cultures also make sure to disparage other cultures, religions and traditions as sources of knowledge and self-reflection. In fact they often ridicule the idea of self-reflection, contrasting it with the idea of absolute truth proclaimed through revelation or the handing down of wisdom from one generation of sages to another. By claiming that the only valid source of knowledge is internal to the group they attempt to lessen the importance of multicultural exchanges and to render them less harmful.

Despite all the attempts illiberal cultures make to stave off the threats posed by multiculturalism, the threats remain. Members of such groups thus feel that they have been forced to join a liberal game, which places liberal values such as pluralism and diversity at its core. Liberals may attempt to present this 'game' as embodying a concession to the demands and needs of members of illiberal groups, but this concession is motivated from within the liberal tradition and its acceptance of a set of beliefs which celebrates the plurality of cultures, ways of life and conceptions of the good. This set of values is, however, external to illiberal traditions which hold a particular, closed, often authoritarian conception of the good life and reject pluralism and diversity. Demanding that such groups open up and respect other ways of life amounts to a demand that they compromise their beliefs and face the risk of assimilation. This suggests that while defenders of liberal cultures have a reason to accept certain compromises in pursuit of a *modus vivendi* with illiberal groups, defenders of illiberal cultures have reasons to reject such compromises.

The recognition that illiberal forces play a significant political role both within liberal democratic states and in the international arena, and the recognition consequently of the need to find ways of communicating with, and if necessary accommodating, these cultures, forces liberals to acknowledge the contextual nature of the liberal political tradition and to seek ways of reaching beyond it. This is a case in which practical necessity reshapes theory; it compels liberals to re-examine their ideological inventory, make good use of their theoretical tools and expose their communal sensitivities. This re-examination allows them to go a long way towards respecting the needs of members of illiberal cultures, but the process cannot be reciprocated, as illiberal cultures do not have the theoretical foundations that would allow them to pay genuine respect to liberal ones. The result is an asymmetric process whereby liberals compromise, for principled reasons, their own principles in an attempt to accommodate illiberal cultures, while illiberal cultures endure liberal cultures merely out of necessity as their own principles do not leave room for a more fundamental type of concession.

So why would members of illiberal cultures adopt the compromises demanded by the idea of multiculturalism? The reason could not be any moral principle, yet it might still be possible to call on their self-interest to support an uneasy truce in preference to all-out war. 'But that will not show that the parties can agree that this is the *right* outcome; rather each side might reasonably reject accommodation if it could win the conflict outright, but will be willing to accept a *modus vivendi* as the second-best solution if the only real alternative is still worse.'[29] If members of illiberal communities are convinced that it is better for them to come to terms with liberal communities and gain protection, respect and representation than to find themselves in a constant state of struggle they might decide to cooperate. This type of argument is, however, contingent on the illiberal community being found in a minority position. Were the community in a position to impose its own ways and values it would do so. The compromise from the point of view of the illiberal community is not even a principled *modus vivendi*, based on a 'live and let live', but a conditional one which is based on fear rather than respect.

The two parties thus have different motivations to enter into an agreement: while its endorsement by liberals is grounded in respect for the lifestyles of others, its endorsement by illiberal cultures is grounded in arguments of lesser evil. Hence the idea of a thick multicultural society raises the following difficulty: if supported by autonomy-based liberalism on the ground that it will allow a gradual and peaceful transformation of all cultures into autonomy-respecting ones, it might be resented and rejected by defenders of illiberal cultures. If, on the other hand, it is supported on the grounds of genuine respect for others, then liberalism is placed on the defensive as it asymmetrically opens itself to illiberal influences.

CONCLUSION

Multicultural debates in a democratic state could lead to an overlapping consensus if they are intra-liberal debates. If, however, both liberal and illiberal cultures are involved, the most one can achieve is a conditional *modus vivendi* based on respect on the part of the liberal cultures and compliance with their position as a minority on the part of the illiberal ones. This suggests that liberals should limit both their demands towards and their expectations of illiberal cultures. This does not commit liberals to cultural relativism; it is merely a requirement of caution, on the part of 'those who make, and above all apply, moral judgements, especially if they are powerful and do so in alien moral cultural contexts'.[30]

These features of thick multiculturalism make it impossible to achieve a political agreement which would be seen as ideal by either of the parties. The most that can be achieved is an untidy compromise which all parties resent to some extent. There is then no right solution, but a set of reasonable ones. Such solutions cannot be defined *a priori* but must be the product of constant political discussions and negotiations. Philosophers thus seem to have little to say about the nature of such agreements and should leave politicians to search for practical solutions.

Does this mean that the theoretical discussions concerning multiculturalism have exhausted themselves? This conclusion is only partly true. In discussing current issues political philosophers hope to analyse an issue in a way that would allow for better understanding of what ought to be done; but they also hope to reflect upon their own concepts, principles and theories. While the contribution of the present debate to the former end might be quite restricted, its contribution to the latter is considerable as it forces political philosophers to look back at the foundation of their own thinking. The phenomena of multiculturalism invite a reconsideration of most of the concepts used in political theory: *membership, boundaries, citizenship, sovereignty, group rights and individual rights, pluralism, toleration, democracy, representation*. No such concept can be used in its traditional guise; they must all be reshaped and re-justified. But most of all multiculturalism demands a redefinition of educational ends and means. This process of self-reflection may, however, reflect back on actual disputes and policies.

It is in this light that the following essays should be read. All the papers in this volume — Lukes' discussion of cultural diversity, Walzer's analysis of multicultural citizenship and democratic education, Mendus' exploration of the limits of toleration, Rorty's view of the virtues of a multicultural curriculum, Macedo's inquiry into the nature and scope of liberal demands and McLaughlin's, Halstead's and Lorberbaum's discussions of religious rights — use multiculturalism to reflect on the liberal democratic tradition and in so doing allow us better to understand its scope as well as its limits.

NOTES AND REFERENCES

1. Raz, J., *Ethics in the Public Domain* (Oxford, Oxford University Press, 1994), p. 69.
2. Walzer, M., Comment, in: A. Gutmann (Ed.) *Multiculturalism and the Politics of Recognition* (Princeton: Princeton University Press, 1992), p. 99.
3. *Ibid.*, p. 99.
4. *Ibid.*, p. 100.
5. Not all cultural minorities desired integration. Some may have recognised from the beginning the implausibility of this ideal. Others wished to retain their identity even at the price of exclusion, or hoped for secessionist arrangements which would allow them to preserve their identity within their own territory.
6. Young, I., Polity and group difference: a critique of the ideal of universal citizenship, *Ethics*, vol. 99, demonstrates how gender issues followed the same pattern.
7. Gutmann (*op. cit.*), p. 12.
8. Young I., *Justice and the Politics of Difference* (Princeton, Princeton University Press, 1990).
9. Young 1989, p. 267.
10. Young *Ibid.*
11. Young *Ibid.*, p. 265.
12. Walzer, M., Education, democratic citizenship and multiculturalism, below, p. 23.
13. Kamm, T., Clash of cultures: rise of Islam in France rattles the populace and stirs backlash, *Wall Street Journal*, 5 January 1995.
14. *Ibid.*
15. *Ibid.*
16. Nagel, T., *Equality and Partiality* (Oxford, Oxford University Press, 1991), p. 169.
17. One could portray this debate differently, as a conflict not between French liberalism and Muslim illiberalism, but between French illiberalism and legitimate Muslim ways of life. The goal of neutrality does not authorise violations of negative liberty such as restricting what garments can be worn. No compromise of liberalism is necessary to allow the wearing of the scarves; indeed liberalism demands such freedoms be respected. Alternatively one could claim that this is an encounter between two illiberal cultures. (I am grateful to Jacob Levi for pointing this out to me.)
18. Rawls, J., The law of peoples, in: S. Shute and S. Hurley (Eds.), *On Human Rights* (New York, Basic Books, 1994), p. 43.
19. Taylor, C., The politics of recognition, in: A. Gutmann (Ed.), *Multiculturalism* (*op. cit.*), p. 57.
20. Raz, J., *The Morality of Freedom* (Oxford: Oxford University Press, 1986), p. 372.
21. *Ibid.*, pp. 423–4.
22. Raz, *op. cit.* 1994, p. 76.
23. Mendus, S., Toleration and recognition: education in a multicultural society, below, p. 33.
24. *Ibid.*
25. Feinberg, W., Liberalism and the aims of multicultural education, below, p. 45.
26. Wringe, C., Educational rights in multicultural democracies, below, p. 127.
27. Halstead, M., Voluntary apartheid? Problems of schooling for religious and other minorities in democratic societies, below, p. 99.
28. Macedo, S., Multiculturalism for the religious right? Defending liberal civic education, below, p. 65.
29. Nagel (*op. cit.*), p. 169.
30. Lukes, S., Moral diversity and relativism, below, p. 15.

Moral Diversity and Relativism

STEVEN LUKES

How should we react to the diversity of morals? What theoretical and practical conclusions should we draw from the ever-more visible contrasts between ways of life — between different practices and customs, between divergent perspectives on life and judgements about what makes it valuable, between divergent ways of responding to common problems that generate countless misunderstandings and conflicts that can end in wars?

This question has not always seemed puzzling. As I shall suggest below, the perception of moral diversity goes back at least to antiquity, whereas the question of how to respond to it is fairly modern. John Locke, for example, observed that 'there is scarce that Principle of Morality to be named, or *Rule of Virtue* to be thought on (those only excepted, that are absolutely necessary to hold Society together, which commonly too are neglected betwixt distinct Societies) which is not, somewhere or other, *slighted* and condemned by the general Fashion of *whole societies* of Men'.[1] Yet Locke did not in consequence doubt that moral principles dictating right action and good government were discoverable, requiring 'Reasoning and Discourse, and some Exercise of the Mind, to discover the Certainty of their Truth'.[2] And when Pascal observed that 'what is truth on one side of the Pyrenées is error on the other',[3] he did not for one moment suppose that this observation required him to put in question the truths delivered by Christianity. 'Mahomet does not prophesy; Jesus prophesies', he wrote. 'No religion other than ours has taught that man is born in sin, no sect of philosophers has said it: none has therefore spoken the truth'.[4]

Religious faith is, indeed, one obvious basis on which the answer to the question I have asked will not seem puzzling or difficult but obvious. Another is that kind of Enlightenment rationalism, of which Locke was a forerunner, according to which the principles of morality can be discerned by the light of Reason, once Humanity has emerged from the darkness of dogma and removed the shadows of superstition. But in our time, when both religious and rationalist certainties are put in doubt, the very fact of moral diversity — both across the world and within our increasingly 'pluralistic' societies — becomes disturbing. Can moral judgements be made across cultural boundaries? Do moral principles apply across divergent ways of life? Do 'our' principles apply to 'them'? Must moral criticism always be internal to a way of life? Is the very idea of a universal morality a pre-postmodern illusion?

Let me begin this enquiry by quoting a well-known passage from Herodotus, which is a favourite reference point in discussions of this set of issues. According to Herodotus, Darius, King of the Persians, took a wisely tolerant view of his subject peoples:

When Darius was King of Persia, he summoned the Greeks who happened to be present at his court, and asked them what they would take to eat the dead bodies of their fathers. They replied that they would not do it for any money in the world. Later, in the presence of the Greeks and through an interpreter (so that they could understand what was said) he asked some Indians, of the tribe called Callatiae, who do in fact eat their parents' dead bodies, what they would take to burn them. They uttered a cry of horror and forbade him to mention such a dreadful thing. One can see by this what custom can do, and Pindar, in my opinion, was right when he called it 'king of all'.[5]

Several morals may be drawn from this familiar story. One I have already indicated: the fact of moral diversity is a very old story. Yet it does now appear differently—and in contradictory ways. On the one hand, it is ever more perceptible and indeed omnipresent. Mass travel and modern mass communications make us all aware, on a daily basis, of the manifold differences between cultures across the world, and of clashes between them—through television documentaries, plays and films and the mere reporting of the news. Mass immigration, trade and professional mobility across frontiers have made our societies ever more heterogeneous and polyglot—Babels of languages, cuisines and customs. Yet we often see these developments through lenses that are themselves shaped by social and political processes. The differences are very often seen as lying between nationally or ethnically or racially defined communities, with the accompanying implication that their cultures are 'wholes', coherent internally and distinct from one another. Many parties have collaborated in shaping this perception: imperialist powers, the politicians and officials of host countries, nationalist movements, populist leaders and intellectuals and, it must be added, social anthropologists in need of unified and uncontaminated objects of study. The idea that cultures are wholes, rather than clusters or assemblages of heterogeneous elements with varying origins, is a systematic exercise in the reduction of complexity based on mythical thinking. Of course, cultures do differ, but, as Mary Midgley has very well put it, 'they differ in a way which is much more like that of climatic regions or ecosystems than it is like the frontiers drawn with a pen between nation states'.[6]

The second moral to be drawn from Herodotus' story is that the various parties involved—the Greeks, the interpreter, the Callatiae, Darius, Herodotus and the reader—all have access to the differences in custom that the story is about. Everyone can understand, from his or her own point of view, that these are different ways of honouring the dead. The Greeks and the Callatiae regard their respective ways of doing this as sacred and the others' way as shocking. Darius, apparently, takes a lofty, detached, sophisticated view of the clash between their views. Yet, as Midgley points out, this is only an appearance, for the Persians 'knew very well that they had solved the problem of disposal in the only *right* way, namely by putting corpses on high towers and letting the vultures eat them'.[7] The reader's view is likely to be similarly tied to conscious or unacknowledged assumptions about how the dead should be honoured—or, at least, to assumptions that are prevalent in his or her society, even if such a reader does not share them. Herodotus, we may assume, took the Greek view of the matter. About the interpreter, sadly, we know nothing.

Thirdly, I believe that this shows that all the parties mentioned above are, in different ways, ethnocentric. Everyone is making sense of the practices in question from his or her own local point of view. The Greeks and the Callatiae are, it seems, doing so unreflectively. They each simply assume that theirs is the only right way and that the others are deeply and shockingly wrong in what they do. Darius, tolerating these eccentric customs like all wise imperialists, understands them as wrong-headed ways of doing what the Persians know how to do properly. The modern reader will understand the eating or burning of one's parents' dead bodies as bizarre and exotic analogues of modern burial practices. If he is an anthropologist, he is likely to bring them under the category of 'ritual' and render them intelligible by comparing them with other funeral rites. In all these cases, the familiar is our point of access to the unfamiliar: eating or burning are 'their' way of paying respect to the dead.

The fourth moral is that making sense of these practices is making *rational* sense of them: that is to say, understanding them as being performed for reasons. Herodotus, following Pindar, says that custom is king of all. It is not entirely clear exactly what he meant. Montaigne said a similar thing in his famous essay on 'Custom'. He wrote that the effect of custom was

> to seize and grip us so firmly, that we are scarce able to escape from its grasp, and to regain possession of ourselves sufficiently to discuss and reason out its commands. In truth, since we imbibe them with our mother's milk, and the world shows the same face to our infant eyes, we seem to be born to follow this same path; and the common ideas that we find around us, and infused into our souls with the seed of our fathers, appear to be general and natural. Whence it comes that what is off the hinges of custom we believe to be off the hinges of reason: God knows how unreasonably for the most part.[8]

Jon Elster has recently given a similar account of apparently irrational customs or social norms as 'to a large extent b'ind and compulsive, mechanical and even unconscious'.[9] If Herodotus meant something like this, then he was wrong, just as Montaigne and Elster are.[10] Of course people often follow customs (norms) blindly, even compulsively and without reasoning about what they do. But the fact that they don't reason does not mean that they don't have reasons. Perhaps, after all, Herodotus' metaphor of custom as king is apposite. When we obey it, custom, like the king, has authority over us: that is, we comply because the norm requires us to do so and we assume there is good reason to do so but do not judge or question it.

Making sense of these ritual practices of the Greeks and the Callatiae is to understand why they do what they do. That must involve grasping their beliefs — about the meaning of death, the powers of ancestors, the powers of the dead over the living and many other cognate matters. Indeed really to understand what is going on will require a pretty comprehensive understanding of their world-views or cosmologies. The moral I seek to draw here is that understanding what they do involves judging what reasons they have for doing what they do — that is to say, judging it to be rational. But there are various possibilities here. We may judge their actions to be rational, *given what they believe*. Or we may judge their actions, given what they believe, to be rational in the light of their purposes or interests or needs which they would acknowledge were they to reflect on these. Or we may interpret or 'decode' their beliefs in such a way as to show them to have good reasons from our perspective: an example of this approach is Robin Horton's interpretation of traditional African medicine, invoking spiritual agencies, as being a sort of proto-scientific explanation appealing to intervening variables.[11] Or we may judge their actions, given what they believe, to be rational in the light of some objective standard, such as, say, the requirements of hygiene.

But — and this is the fifth moral — moral matters are not like matters of hygiene. There is no objective point of view or 'view from nowhere' such that all reasonable persons (from all cultural backgrounds) can be brought to agree on, say, how the dead should be honoured, or, indeed, whether they should be honoured at all, or on the importance of respecting ancestors or on what are fit objects of reverence and admiration or indignation and outrage. In this sense, the right way to honour one's dead parents is relative to culture and context.

I now want to address the question asked at the beginning more generally by suggesting that there are three kinds of answer to it — the ethnocentric, the rationalist and the relativist. My view is that there is, in principle, a reasonable and convincing version of each and that these may be combined into a single plausible answer to the question we are discussing. I shall not address a fourth possible answer — that which appeals to religious faith — partly because I have nothing useful to say about it, and partly because I believe that it in part overlaps with the first answer.

The ethnocentric reaction to moral diversity can take several forms. The Greeks and the Callatiae in Herodotus' story stand for the straightforward, simple, unreflective variety: our beliefs and practices are sacred; the rest of the world is either damned or to be saved. In the modern world religious sects are inclined to this embattled view. I suppose it is also characteristic of what is called 'fundamentalism'. Darius parhaps stands for the imperialist variety: keep the barbarians in their places.

There are many other, more reflective, variants. The history of social anthropology, for example, is replete with arguments about how to construe the divide between modern, Western societies and non-modern, non-Western ones, or indeed about whether there is such a divide. In these discussions it is standard practice to label as ethnocentric those writers who assume modern, Western superiority in one or another sphere — cognitive, technical, moral and so on. The evolutionist and intellectualist anthropologists of the nineteenth century assumed that the 'savages' or, later, 'primitive' societies failed by 'our' standards; their magic was failed or proto-science, their religions nature or animistic myths or a kind of proto-sociology, as Durkheim thought. But there has been another, closely related debate, among anthropologists and elsewhere, that has its origins in the eighteenth century. Do the differences between the moralities or 'moeurs' of different societies or cultures go deep or do they simply mark superficial differences that mask an unchanging set of human capacities and dispositions? Was Hume right in thinking that 'mankind is much the same in all times and places'? This remains a deep question: how and where to identify 'human nature' across the diversity of cultures. Rousseau pinpointed this problem most acutely when he observed that

For all the three or four hundred years that the inhabitants of Europe have inundated other parts of the world and ceaselessly published new accounts of voyages and relations, I am persuaded that when we learn about men we are learning about Europeans.[12]

The task, he thought, was to 'cast away the yoke of national prejudices, learn to understand men by their conformities and their differences and learn to acquire universal knowledge that is not that of one century or one country exclusively'. To study men, one must 'look close by'; to study man one must 'learn to adopt the view from afar: one must first observe the differences in order to discover (his) properties'.[13]

The 'yoke of national prejudices' is a good description of ethnocentrism and in matters of morality it must, of course, be cast away, so far as is possible, when we are seeking to understand and to live with those who live by other moralities than our own. Yet there is, I think, a sense in which ethnocentricity is inescapable, to which I have already alluded in discussing Herodotus' story. We can, in the end, only understand the unfamiliar by analogy with the familiar. The important thing is to extend the range of the latter and to discipline the processes of understanding by the use of rigorous and relevant comparative methods.

The 'rationalist' reaction to moral diversity is essentially the idea that it is possible through ratiocination, through reasoning and discourse and some exercise of the mind, to arrive at firm conclusions about the right and the good that will be universally valid, applicable to all mankind and acceptable to all reasonable persons after due reflection. It is an old dream which has, many argue, led in practice to many real nightmares. In modern times it is instantiated in both the Kantian and the Utilitarian traditions of moral theory. In its strong and pure version, just stated, it is hard to accept today.

The rationalist reaction need not necessarily be ethnocentric, though it very often is. It is entirely possible to hold that rational principles of moral and political life have most closely incarnated in some past or remote present society or in some imagined future. In the eighteenth and nineteenth centuries it tended to take an evolutionist form, as in the thought of Condorcet or Saint-Simon and Comte, Bentham and Mill. It is hard to believe any longer in such theories of moral progress, even if they incorporate some notion of the 'cunning of reason' that takes regressive bypasses that lead nevertheless in the end to the perfect social and moral order.

Rationalism in the late twentieth century must needs be sceptical. It is, to say the least, no longer fashionable to proclaim with Condorcet that one seeks 'a form of government that is good by its very nature, founded on principles that are sure, absolute, universal, independent of times and places'.[14] Foundationalism, absolutes and claims to moral universality have become suspect in virtually all departments of contemporary culture.

Nevertheless, it is neither easy nor wise to allow justified suspicions to lead one into moral nihilism. It is not easy once one reflects that moral thinking is, in large part, moral reasoning, and reasoning involves invoking and giving reasons. Reasons are available to all who can reason and cannot be completely internal to a particular way of life or culture. In any case, as suggested above, cultures are not seamless wholes and incorporate within them practices of criticism and reasoning. And morality itself is a way of reasoning through which customs are maintained, developed and sometimes rejected or abandoned. It is not wise, since to abandon the idea that moral reasoning can lead to conclusions that can convince the reasonable is to abandon the very practice of moral criticism which is an inherent feature of our own moral tradition: it is thus to cease to take our own morality seriously. What survives of the rationalist response is, I believe, the project of responding to moral diversity (which John Rawls calls the 'fact of pluralism') by moral and political argument that takes as little for granted as is possible: that does not assume the value of any particular way of life or the justice of any particular set of social and political arrangements.

The standard contemporary objection to such a response underlies the third kind of reaction to moral diversity I wish to mention: the relativist reaction. This is the view that moral principles and judgements are only valid internally within particular cultures. Once again, there are different versions. There is the doctrine favoured by the school of thought called 'cultural relativism' that each culture is valid in its own terms, that its norms and principles are only applicable within, that to understand means not to criticise. Alternatively, there is the sceptical view that, for epistemological or other reasons, judgements cannot be made across cultural boundaries: 'they' cannot be judged by 'our' standards. Such views are very popular these days and have many motivational sources: hostility to or guilt about ethnocentrism, especially of the imperialist variety, an ill-thought-out interpretation of the principle of equal recognition or respect in multicultural societies, a romantic hostility to what is seen as abstract rationalism, and doubtless other resistible temptations.

What is wrong with such views should already be largely apparent from what has been said above. First there is the mythical assumption of 'cultural wholes': it is never clear — nor can it be — to what supposedly coherent unities moral principles and judgements are supposed to be relative, who is an insider and who is an outsider. Second, these views cannot account for the practice of moral criticism within cultures and across them. Are cruel and unjust practices uncriticisable just because others practise them? And what if deviants or rebels or intellectuals criticise the practices of their own societies? Are they following the local practice (of criticism) or making impermissible judgements? And may others not criticise us? Third, is it really a form of respect to abstain from criticising the practices of others, thereby regarding them as beyond or beneath criticism? And fourth, what is the status of these relativist views themselves: are they valid across cultures or only relative to one? And fifth, the relativist reaction to the plurality of moralities misconceives that very plurality for it eliminates conflict. The problem with which we began is, in large part, a problem for us because different forms of life yield answers to moral questions that conflict. The trouble with relativism is that it purports to eliminate the conflict. If each answer is true in its own place, none can clash.

Yet despite all these and other well-known objections, there is a surviving truth in moral relativism, if it is modestly construed in the spirit of Montaigne, as a requirement of caution on those who make, and above all apply, moral judgements, especially if they are powerful and do so in alien moral cultural contexts. Understood in this way, the relativist reaction to moral diversity can serve as an antidote to the dangers of hasty and overbearing ethnocentrism and abstract rationalistic moralising. I have argued that, in a certain sense, ethnocentrism is methodologically inevitable, but in the service of the relativist's ambition of revealing the rationality of the actors' world from within.

NOTES AND REFERENCES

1. J. Locke, *An Essay concerning Human Understanding*, 1, iii, 10.
2. *Ibid.*, 1, iii, 1.
3. B. Pascal, *Pensées*, 294.
4. *Ibid.*, 599, 606.
5. Herodotus, *Histories*, Book III, Ch. 38.
6. M. Midgley, *Can't We Make Moral Judgments?* (Bristol: The Bristol Press, 1991), p. 84.
7. *Ibid.*, p. 78.
8. *The Essays of Montaigne* translated by E. Trechmann (London: Oxford University Press, 1927), 2 vols.; essay no. 23: 'Of Custom', Vol. 1, p. 111.
9. J. Elster, *The Cement of Society: A Study of Social Order* (Cambridge, Cambridge University Press, 1989), p. 100.
10. See my article, The rationality of norms, *Archives Européennes de Sociologie*, 32, 1 (1991), pp. 142–149.
11. R. Horton, African traditional thought and Western science, in B. R. Wilson, ed., *Rationality* (Oxford: Blackwell, 1970), pp. 131–171.
12. J.-J. Rousseau, *Discours sur l'origine de l'inégalité*, in: *Oeuvres Complètes* (Paris: Gallimard-Pléiade, 1959–1969), vol. 3, p. 212.
13. *Ibid.*, p. 213 and *Essai sur les origines des langues* (Bordeaux: Ducros, 1968), p. 89.
14. M.J.A.N. de Condorcet, *Oeuvres*, 1847–1849, vol. 4, p. 275.

Education, Democratic Citizenship and Multiculturalism

MICHAEL WALZER

I

Arguments about democratic citizenship and education in a multicultural setting have to begin with a description of the setting. I don't mean only a list of the different cultural groups or a report on the last census (how many identified members of each group?) or a map of their residential concentrations or dispersions. We also need an account of the history that produced this specific assortment of 'cultures' and of the institutional arrangements that have determined the character of their co-existence. Obviously, this account must be particularised, focused on *these* groups, co-existing in *this* time and place. But I want to begin with three ideal-typical accounts. For reasons that will soon become apparent, I shall turn to the particularities of Israeli multiculturalism only after presenting these three.

The first institutional history is that of the old empires and (some of) their successor states. Here the different cultural groups — nations and religious communities — were brought together through an *ad hoc* process of dynastic expansion: conquest, purchase, marriage and so on. Sometimes the imperial élite tried to impose its own language and culture on all its subjects (Czarist Russification is the most obvious example), but more often it was content to divide and rule — that is, to maintain the different groups in their differences, allowing them considerable autonomy in exchange for their acceptance of imperial hegemony. Thus there developed the millet system of the Ottomans, for which we could find many analogues in ancient Persia and Rome, in medieval Europe, in the various caliphates of the Islamic world, and in the European colonial empires.[1] Autonomy is by no means a singular arrangement: it takes very different forms. It can be regional or functional in character; it can encompass a wider or narrower range of communal activities; it can extend or not extend to the use of coercive power (including capital punishment). But it does have a singular effect: it gives legal standing to the various groups and so requires individuals to identify themselves with one or another of the groups and submit to its laws — most particularly in matters of family life, marriage, divorce, inheritance and so on; often also in matters of education.

The second institutional history is that of the modern nation-state, which virtually always incorporates a number of 'national minorities'. Nation-states have been variously formed, sometimes through long-term processes of consolidation (France, Italy, Germany), sometimes through partition (Pakistan), sometimes through liberationist or secessionist struggles against the old empires—all of these carried out under the aegis of a nationalist ideology, asserting the right of this group of people to govern themselves in accordance with their own history and culture, in their own 'homeland'. National minorities are simply smaller groups, usually associated with majorities elsewhere, whose members find themselves—so they are likely to think—on the wrong side of the border when the border is finally drawn. They now encounter a state that reflects and upholds the culture of the majority nation, making its language the language of public affairs, enforcing its calendar, celebrating its holidays, teaching its history in the public schools. Minorities sustain themselves as best they can in their families and voluntary associations. The state is sometimes tolerant and even supportive of these efforts, sometimes not. In either case, its aim is the cultural survival and well-being of the majority, while it makes no strong commitment to the survival of minority cultures.

The third institutional history is that of immigrant societies (the United States is only one among a number of cases, though I will draw upon its example in the account that follows). These societies take shape through the arrival of settlers, one by one or family by family, gradually displacing or subordinating an indigenous population. Perhaps one national group is dominant early on, the first settlers coming from the same 'old country', but this dominance is unstable given a continuous flow of immigrants. Soon there are many 'old countries' and many immigrant cultures in the new land. The state is forced into a kind of neutrality, which is first expressed in religious toleration and secularism and then in a slow disengagement from the national history and cultural style of the first immigrants. The disengagement is always partial and incomplete, which means that some newcomers find the public life of the country more familiar and congenial than others. Nonetheless, in principle, all the immigrants, including the first ones, must sustain their religious and cultural life, their national memories and customs, by themselves: the state is committed to none of them. It celebrates only its own history, creates its own holidays, and teaches in its public schools the general values of toleration, neutrality, mutual respect and so on—not the particular values of any of the groups its citizens form.[2]

To each of these three institutional histories there corresponds an (ideal-typical) set of educational arrangements. In the old empires, barring 'Russification' programmes, each of the autonomous communities organised its own schools and planned its own curriculum—sometimes with public support and one or another degree of public regulation. The successor states are likely to be wary of so radical a decentralisation, taking education as one of their own prerogatives. But they, too, insofar as they are still nationally or religiously pluralist in character, must plan different curricula for the different communities or allow them some room for the teaching of their own history and culture. The language of instruction, at least for some part of the curriculum, will be the communal language, even if the language of the political centre is required more generally.

Nation-states, by contrast, impose a national curriculum and a national language (France provides the best example of this: the Minister of Education is said to know at any moment in time what every schoolchild is reading). A

unified school system presses a single history and culture upon its students —
even if it rarely reaches to the radical curriculum proposed by Rousseau, who
held that nothing but this single history and culture should be studied.[3]
Minority cultures socialise their children at home or in private schools or
after-school programmes. In immigrant societies there is also likely to be a
single public school system, which ignores all the constituent cultures or
struggles, in the contemporary multicultural fashion, to give equal time and
space to each of them. Many national and religious communities, the latter
especially, run their own schools in competition with the public system or in
addition to it, imposing extra hours of education upon their children.

II

These are ideal-typical accounts, as I have said, but Israel's specificity consists
in the fact that it partakes in all of them. The pattern of its internal differences
is highly complex because it is constituted by all three of these different
institutional histories. Israel is triply divided. First of all, it is one of the
successor states of the Ottoman Empire (the succession mediated by the British
Empire), and it has retained the millet system for its various religious
communities, allowing them to run their own courts and providing a (partially)
differentiated set of educational programmes in two languages. Secondly, Israel
is a modern nation-state, established by a nationalist movement, and
incorporating a substantial 'national minority'. Members of the minority are
citizens of the state, but they do not find their culture or history mirrored in its
public life. And, thirdly, Israel's Jewish majority is a society of immigrants,
drawn from every part of a widely scattered diaspora, an 'ingathering' of men
and women who have in fact, despite their common Jewishness (itself
sometimes subject to dispute), very different histories and cultures.
Educational arrangements reflect this complexity, so that the schools have
different and not entirely consistent aims: sustaining differences, both religious
and national in origin; fostering a single national (Zionist or Israeli)
consciousness; and incorporating and naturalising immigrants, teaching
mutual respect and self-respect.

No doubt, other countries enjoy or endure other sorts of complexity. But this
combination of histories and institutions makes for an extraordinary
intensification of difference among what is after all a fairly small population
occupying a fairly small space: three religions (corporately organised, though
each of them is in fact divided into subgroups); two nations; and many
ethnicities. Since no one is likely to claim that these differences can be overcome
or transcended, it is necessary to think of ways of living with them. In the
United States, many people believe that all the immigrants will eventually
become 'Americans', forging a single identity through residential dispersion
and social inter-mixing and inter-marriage. Perhaps the same thing will happen
to Jewish immigrants to Israel, Ashkenazim and Sephardim, Latin Americans,
Moroccans, Russians, and Ethiopians emerging one day as Israeli Jews simply.
But the long-established on-the-ground national and religious differences will
not go away, not even over the long haul. How can they, then, be
accommodated?

The only thing that all the different groups share is a common citizenship. They vote in the same elections; they obey the same laws (except for family law); they pay the same taxes; they participate in the same arguments about what the state should and should not do. Because Israel is a democratic society, the way is open for what might be called a 'strong' citizenship, and indeed the rates of political participation and the levels of political understanding, among all the different communities, are quite high relative to other democracies.[4] The quarrels that difference generates have, so far at least, strengthened political commitment rather than producing alienation and withdrawal. So there is this commonality to work with — and the work is urgently necessary. Commonality has to be fostered and enhanced, because the same differences that make for political commitment also make for intolerance and zeal. No doubt, these latter qualities are intensified by Israel's international environment, but they have much to feed on at home. There are so many people towards whom one can be intolerant: ethnically, even racially, different Jews; secular and religious Jews; secular and religious Muslims; Christians, Muslims and Jews; Arabs, Druse, Circassians, Armenians . . . and Jews again. Can it be any help that all these people are also Israeli citizens?

Certainly, the democratic arena is very different from civil society with its multiple divisions. Even if political parties reflect social differences, they are at the same time driven by the logic of the arena to look for votes wherever they can find them — and then in the bargaining that follows the voting to make whatever deals are necessary in order to form a government. No one can govern without soliciting votes from the body of citizens, each of whom has only one to offer. If a narrowly ideological (religious or nationalist) partly focuses on a single group of voters, it cannot enter a government without negotiating with other parties differently focused. If it does not compromise its ideology in order to win votes, it must do so in the search for coalition partners. However difference is marked off in civil society, it must be bridged in the political arena.[5]

If we are interested in co-existence, then, the arena is a good place, despite all the shouting that goes on within it — and it could be a better place if the noise level were kept down. What that requires is simply (or not so simply) that the participants, all the activists and militants and their more passive, but no less opinionated, followers learn to think of one another as *fellow* citizens and to accord to one another the rights that democratic citizenship entails. They do not have to like their fellow citizens or attach any high value to their traditions, practices and opinions. The fellowship of citizens does not have to be particularly warm. It is an alternative to, not an expression of, communal solidarity. We can hope that political participation will create over time a sense of mutual attachment, the recognition of common interests, even some degree of patriotic pride. But all this will come, if it comes, *over time*, the result of a process we might best think of as educational.

But the success of this process cannot depend only on adult education, which is notoriously chancy. Adults, I suppose, are at the lower end of the learning curve; they have learned a lot already, and much of what they have learned does not help them to function within a fellowship of citizens. Democratic education must begin with children. That is chancy, too; we probably have less faith today than we once did in the effectiveness of schools. Children learn from their parents, and from their peers, and from the mass media, as much as, perhaps more than, they learn from their teachers. But they do learn something from their teachers, and so we have to pay attention to what the teachers teach. What should be required in an education for democratic citizenship?

III

I shall assume the existence of segregated schools on roughly the present Israeli model — that is, with national and religious groups largely separated and the various Jewish ethnicities integrated (except insofar as they are divided by religious and secular commitments). I leave aside class divisions, since the story I want to tell is complicated enough. Democratic education is probably best carried on in integrated schools, which anticipate the integration of the political arena. But a multiply divided society with a complex imperial/nationalist/ immigrant history is unlikely to achieve anything like a full-scale integration, not now, when all the histories are, as it were, immediate and resonant, and not in the foreseeable future. Any effort in that direction would only outrage the constituent communities, each of which seeks to control, so far as it is able, the education of its own children. If it cannot shape the curriculum entirely to its wishes, it will still insist that whatever is taught be taught to *this* cohesive group of children — setting limits, that is, on personal if not mental associations. How else can communal survival be guaranteed?

So, every cluster of segregated schools will aspire to reach a particular set of students and teach them a particular history, culture, religion and so on. Multiculturalism will then be a feature of the educational system as a whole, not necessarily of any particular school — though the world of secular liberals and leftists, committed in principle to pluralism, might generate a more local multiculturalism (in practice, Israeli secular liberals and leftists appear to learn very little about the life of religious Muslims or Jews). There are certainly good reasons to insist that all the students in all the schools should be taught something about the 'others', their fellow citizens, but it seems to me even more important that they be taught, first of all, something about citizenship itself.[6]

A common civic curriculum is necessary (and therefore ought to be legally required) for two reasons: because the state also has to do what it can to guarantee its survival, to produce and reproduce citizens, to ensure that the various particularist identities co-exist with a more general identity; and because this more general identity provides the best possible motive for a sympathetic understanding of the various particularisms. Democratic citizenship in a divided society makes for a politics of difference, and people who come to value this kind of politics will, one can hope, want to know something about the differences that it encompasses.

The civic curriculum itself will not be multicultural — though when it is introduced into nationally or religiously focused schools, it may well represent the first suggestion of a different way of life. For democratic citizenship is not a neutral idea; it has its own particular history, and it points towards its own (political) culture. No doubt, its study will more easily be accommodated by some schools than by others. It is more likely to be resisted by some teachers than by others. A serious education in the commonalities of citizenship will require an uncommon political struggle; state officials will have to use their coercive powers—above all, but not only, the power of the purse. Now, what is it that they should insist on? Obviously, they must not be satisfied with some innocuous and soporific course in good government. Much more is necessary; I would suggest three critical requirements.

First, a *history* of democratic institutions and practices from ancient Greece forwards—and, alongside this, an honest engagement with the Jewish (and Muslim) predilection for non-democratic forms of government. It is, I suppose, difficult to determine just how honest this engagement ought to be. Consider, for example, the argument of a number of Zionist scholars, seeking to construct the best possible national history, that the government of ancient Israel, before the monarchy, was a 'primitive democracy' of tribal elders.[7] This is not a claim, it seems to me, that can withstand critical scrutiny, but it is, as such things go, relatively harmless. If it makes possible what we might think of as the naturalisation of democracy within a tradition that otherwise favours the rule of kings or priests or sages, why not include it in the curriculum? I am inclined to prefer the critical scrutiny: include the argument about the elders only if one also includes the counter-argument denying their 'democratic' character. After all, democracy is a culture of criticism and disagreement. There are different ways by which students can be made to feel at home in such a culture, and the claim that we have always lived there is not necessarily the best way. That said, I do not think it is wrong to tell the Jewish story (or the Muslim story) in a revised version, so to speak, that stresses points of access for a democratic understanding. But one must also tell the Greek story and insist on the genuinely formative moments in the history of democracy.

The second critical requirement of the course is a *philosophy* or political theory of democratic government, with all the standard arguments, critically reviewed. In a relatively new country like Israel, where crucially important constitutional questions are still undecided (what should the electoral system be like? should there be a bill of rights?), students should study not only the alternatives to democracy but also the different versions of democracy—and the arguments for and against each one. But the philosophy of democratic government does not stop at the analysis of constitutional arrangements. It extends to practices and attitudes: debate, compromise, tolerance of disagreement, scepticism about authority and so on. I do not know how one teaches such things, especially when it is not possible to count on reinforcement from outside the school. Certainly, a single course, however well-designed, will not do the job. A certain democratic consciousness—open, questioning, hostile to dogmatism—must be at work in every course. But this is not an easy requirement when schools are organised for the sake of religious or, for that matter, ideologically secular instruction. So there also has to be a specific place and time for students to discuss the texts in which a democratic consciousness was first exemplified and defended.

The third requirement is a *practical political science* of democracy: how-to-do-it for citizens, where the everyday working of government ministries, representative assemblies, courts, parties, social movements and so on are studied. This is probably the least controversial part of a democratic education, and also the easiest, since in this case, though not in the others, instruction in school is seconded by the daily news. But there is nonetheless important educational work to be done here: to teach students to think of themselves as future participants, not merely as more or less sophisticated spectators. The spectacle, no doubt, is often unedifying, so teachers must stress that it is in the nature of democracy that the system is never closed. There are always opportunities for people with new or different ideas about how things might be done. Students should be encouraged to experiment with political ideas and taught how to defend them in front of their peers.[8]

IV

I have already suggested that a democratic education of this sort is likely to sit more easily with some of Israel's constituent communities than with others. Democracy has a substantive character; it is not a neutral procedure but a way of life. Now I need to address a more specific question: to what extent does this way of life, in its Israeli version, reflect the dominant cultures of Israeli society—Zionist, Jewish, Ashkenazi—so that all the other cultures must either reject democracy or transform themselves for its sake? Is the democratic education that I have just described (really) a programme for cultural subordination?

It can hardly be denied that Israeli politics reflects the dominant cultures. Democracy as it is now organised has its beginnings in the Zionist Congress and in the *Yishuv*, where Arabs, obviously, had no place and Sephardic Jews were only minimally represented.[9] The state calendar is shaped by the Jewish, not the Christian or Muslim, calendar; state symbols and ceremonies derive from Jewish history. The political élite is still recruited largely from European immigrants and their children. Democracy was an early commitment of these people, even if they came from countries with little experience of democratic government, and the defence of democracy now looks very much like self-defence.

But democratic politics has a logic of its own, which is not subject to the control of its (temporarily) dominant groups. Even conceived as a way of life, which in some sense 'belongs' to the people whose way of life it is, democracy can never be the exclusive possession of an ethnic group or a social class or any subset of the body of citizens. It is permanently open to what we might think of as friendly take-overs (insofar as the citizens are friends, at least in Aristotle's sense, which does not rule out the antagonism of political competition). Of course, it can only be taken over by people who learn the rules, and the take-over can only be called friendly if these same people have internalised the culture of democracy. And is not this a kind of assimilation—cultural loss as well as gain? Democratic schooling (practice too), if it works, will make for assimilation; I see no point in pretending that it will not entail significant changes especially in the various religious cultures of Israeli society. But once the give-and-take of democratic politics is opened up to everyone's giving and taking, even the dominant groups are unlikely to emerge unchanged. Their survival-as-they-are cannot be guaranteed. Political co-existence and interaction will erode the boundaries that divide them from the others; they will have to share power, and even surrender it. Democracy itself, assuming its survival, will appear in new versions, more plebeian, perhaps, or more populist, or more pious.

At the same time, it would be a mistake to overestimate the changes that democratic politics requires from (or imposes on) non-democratic and pre-democratic cultures. Modern societies are sufficiently compartmentalised, their individual members are sufficiently divided, to make it entirely possible, say, for orthodox Jews to elect their Knesset representatives without modifying in any way their loyalty to non-elected sages. Obviously, the potential will now exist for a rival orthodox leadership (though probably not for a rival orthodoxy), and a new, more public, more accessible argument will begin. But traditional authority structures have considerable staying power: rabbis, priests, mullahs, old families, local notables all continue to shape communal opinion long after modernity has called into being a host of eager successors. So there is no reason why democratic politics cannot co-exist with a genuine and vital multiculturalism even if it is not equally in tune, as it were, with all the cultures. And we can help individuals from the different cultures to feel at home in the democratic arena without turning them into strangers in their own families or heretics in their religious communities.

But democracy is still, always, a politics of strain. One wins and loses, takes responsibility for governing without ever having power enough, lives for years in opposition, compromises one's deepest commitments, co-exists with people one does not like or trust. I suppose that the strain must be especially great in multiply divided societies where some political leaders are struggling to build a consensus while others are firing up and mobilising their own particularist constituencies. The politics of difference is both a product of democracy and a danger to it. That is why education is so important—school learning (also practical experience) aimed at producing the patience, stamina, tolerance, and receptiveness without which the strain will not be understood or accepted.

For it is always possible to escape the democratic arena, to hide in the closeness of one's own community, to surrender the responsibilities of citizenship and allow a small political élite to negotiate communal differences or a charismatic leader to override them. We know that multiculturalism can 'work' in authoritarian regimes, as it worked in the old empires before the appearance of nationalist movements and successor states committed, at least in principle, to popular self-rule. Making it work democratically is a relatively new project, an experiment whose real subjects are our children and grandchildren. The point of a democratic education is to give them a fighting chance of success.

NOTES AND REFERENCES

1. For a detailed account of how autonomy worked in medieval Islam, see S. D. Goitein, *A Mediterranean Society*, vol. II, *The Community* (Berkeley: University of California Press, 1971), especially pp. 311ff. On autonomy in the Ottoman Empire, see Bernard Lewis, *The Jews of Islam* (Princeton: Princeton University Press, 1984), pp. 125 ff. (on the millet system).
2. For the American experience, see Michael Walzer, *What It Means to be an American* (New York: Marsilio, 1993).

3. Jean-Jacques Rousseau, *The Government of Poland*, trans. Willmoore Kendall (Indianapolis: Bobbs-Merrill, 1972), chapter IV (Education).

4. For example, in the pivotal election of 1977, the turn-out among all Israeli citizens was 79.2% of eligible voters; in Arab cities, it was 77.4%. *Israel at the Polls*, ed. Howard R. Penniman (Washington, D. C.: American Enterprise Institute, 1979), pp. 63, 65.

5. No Arab party has yet been invited to join a government coalition, but the current government (1995) depends on Arab votes in the Knesset and bargains for them much as it does for the support of its actual partners.

6. For an account of Arab-Jewish division and mutual ignorance, see Michael Romann and Alex Weingrod, *Living Together Separately: Arabs and Jews in Contemporary Jerusalem* (Princeton: Princeton University Press, 1991). The situation of religious and secular Jews is similar to that described there. And the schools have little chance of changing what residence, daily life and politics so consistently confirm.

7. Yehezkel Kaufmann, *The Religion of Israel*, trans. and abridged by Moshe Greenberg (Chicago: University of Chicago Press, 1960), p. 256.

8. For further arguments about and proposals for the education of citizens, see Amy Gutmann, *Democratic Education* (Princeton: Princeton University Press, 1987) and Benjamin Barber, *An Aristocracy for Everyone: The Politics of Education and the Future of America* (New York: Ballantine, 1992).

9. See Dan Horowitz and Moshe Lissak, *Origins of the Israeli Polity* (Chicago: University of Chicago Press, 1978).

Toleration and Recognition: education in a multicultural society

SUSAN MENDUS

The question which informs this paper is 'How, in multicultural and democratic societies, can we educate children in a way which both acknowledges their cultural identity and instils democratic values in them?' To answer this question we need first to understand why there might be a tension between democratic values and the recognition of ethnic or cultural identity. Two writers have recently drawn attention to areas in which conflict can arise. In *Market, State and Community* David Miller notes that the loyalties required for active citizenship in a democratic society such as Britain may conflict with loyalty to an ethnic or cultural group, and he argues that when that happens 'political education must try to shape cultural identities in the direction of common citizenship. It must try to present an interpretation of, let us say, Indian culture, which makes it possible for members of the Indian community to feel at home in and loyal to, the British state. In so far as there are elements in Indian culture which are at odds with such a reconciliation, the interpretation must be selective or, if you like, biased'.[1]

So expressed, Miller's formulation is puzzlingly abstract, and it is difficult to know what exactly he has in mind here. His main argument is that specifically *national* identity, in this case British identity, must take priority over cultural loyalty, but in saying this he gestures towards the more general problem of reconciling the values of cultural communities with the values of democratic citizenship, for we must suppose that part of what is involved in being British is having at least some commitment to the kinds of democratic processes characteristic of a Western liberal society. And there are some cultural communities which lack this commitment, or at any rate are reluctant to extend it to all members of the community. For example, in some cultures the role and status accorded to women is such as to render problematic their education for active citizenship in a democratic state: it is, or may be, thought fitting for women to display the virtue of obedience, but a highly developed sense of obedience, a willingness to accept the word of those in authority, fits ill with being an active citizen in a democratic society such as Britain. Where such conflict occurs, Miller argues, cultural loyalty must take second place to citizen loyalty, and the values of the cultural community must be 'reinterpreted' in a way which lessens the tension between it and citizen identity. For Miller, then, citizen identity trumps cultural identity, and insofar as multicultural education draws attention to values which are at odds with the development of citizen identity (values such as unquestioning obedience), it is to be treated with great caution.

A second approach is to be found in Charles Taylor's book, *Multiculturalism and the Politics of Recognition*. Taylor is concerned with the content rather than the aim of education, and his central question is whether, in a multicultural society, the syllabus ought to be enlarged beyond the traditional 'canon' of great works so as to develop, for example, Afrocentric curricula for mainly black schools. He argues (with some reservations) that it should, and his reason is that it is only by such a strategy that hitherto excluded groups may be given due recognition: 'dominant groups tend to entrench their hegemony by inculcating an image of inferiority in the subjugated. The struggle for freedom and equality must therefore pass through a revision of these images. Multicultural curricula are meant to help in the process of revision'.[2]

So where Miller sees cultural loyalty as a potential threat to common citizenship, Taylor sees it as an important step in the development of self-respect among members of minority groups: a step without which they are doomed to remain inferior in their own eyes and unacknowledged in the eyes of others. Put differently, where Miller sees cultural loyalty as potentially disabling for citizens of a democratic society, Taylor sees cultural recognition as the precondition of a society in which the democratic ideal of equality can be realised.

It would be unwise to exaggerate the differences between these two writers: Miller is no ruthless suppressor of cultural identity. On the contrary, he is anxious to enable members of minority groups to retain a sense of their own cultural identity, but (and it is a big 'but') only insofar as that does not conflict with the requirements of common citizenship. Similarly, Taylor is no naive evangelist for multiculturalism. Recognising the difficulties inherent in supposing that all cultures deserve equal respect, he urges that this be accepted only as a 'presumption', and one which itself has homogenising and colonising tendencies, since it implies that we already have the standards by which to judge that 'their' culture is as good as ours.[3] Nevertheless, their different responses highlight the problems inherent in answering the practical question which forms the topic of this paper: how can we educate people in a way which both respects their cultural identity and fits them for citizenship in a democratic society? Crudely put, the problem is to say how we can acknowledge cultural identity without condoning cultural immurement, or, from the other direction, how we can assert the value of citizen loyalty without driving out cultural loyalty.

In what follows I shall suggest that these problems may be less acute than they at first appear, but solving (or dissolving) them depends upon adopting an understanding of educational aims which is both clearer than and different from the aims implied by Miller and Taylor. So I will try to show that if we understand the purposes of education aright, we need not be forced to choose between citizen identity and cultural loyalty. Or, at least, that those hard choices will be far less frequent than is often supposed.

THE AIMS OF EDUCATION

I begin with Taylor. His preference for an enlarged canon springs from his belief that self-recognition is a *sine qua non* of flourishing in modern society.

But self-recognition includes receiving recognition from others and this, he says, cannot be attained where the excluded culture remains excluded. Thus 'the reason for these proposed changes is not, or not mainly, that all students may be missing something important through the exclusion of a certain gender or certain races, or certain cultures, but rather that women and students from the excluded group are given, either directly or by omission, a demeaning picture of themselves, as though all creativity and worth inhered in males of European provenance. Enlarging and changing the curriculum is therefore essential not so much in the name of a broader culture for everyone as in order to give recognition to the hitherto excluded'.[4]

This argument contains some important assumptions about the aims of education and it is worth dwelling on it for a little while. In the first place, Taylor is not making claims about the objective importance of works currently excluded from the canon. They may or may not be great literature or great works of art, but their inclusion is to be justified not by their inherent worth, but by appeal to the needs of the (hitherto) excluded. Of course, and as Taylor himself points out, there is a potential problem here: members of excluded groups may interpret his strategy as at root patronising, as equivalent to saying 'your culture contains nothing to equal ours, but we will change the curriculum in order that your culture, inferior though it is, may nevertheless be represented'. To guard against this, he proposes that we work with a 'presumption of equal worth' among cultures. This presumption will allow for the recognition of previously excluded groups without degenerating either into cultural relativism or condescension. As a presumption of *equal worth*, it gives recognition to others, but as merely a *presumption* of equal worth it does not imply cultural relativism and the complete rejection of standards. Thus it constitutes a mid-point between cultural immurement and cultural imperialism.[5]

One thing, however, which the account omits is any statement of how an enlarged canon may benefit members of the majority as well as members of the excluded group. As Taylor presents the matter, we are faced with a choice between the claim that enlargement is justified as a pragmatic device for enabling the minority to obtain recognition, and the claim that enlargement is justified by the objective worth of what was previously excluded. But there is a third possibility, which is that enlargement is justified as a means of facilitating recognition in both the minority group and the majority group—in both the hitherto excluded and the hitherto included. If enlargement enables the excluded to understand and value themselves, it should also enable the included to understand and value themselves *by comparison with the excluded*. My suggestion therefore is that we should see education as, quite generally, a means of enabling *all* students to understand themselves. There is nothing particularly new (indeed nothing new at all) in this suggestion, but it does require careful explication if it is to do the philosophical work I require of it, so I turn now to some interpretations of the claim.

On one, very familiar, interpretation of the claim, education enables us to understand ourselves by encouraging and facilitating the development of individual autonomy. We come to understand ourselves by recognising what we as individuals want and value, as distinct from what those around us (our parents, our friends, our colleagues) want and value. This is most eloquently expressed by Saul Bellow in his preface to Allan Bloom's cult book, *The Closing of the American Mind*. Bellow writes:

> As a mid-Westerner, the son of immigrant parents, I recognised at an early age that I was called upon to decide for myself to what extent my Jewish origins, my surroundings (the accidental circumstances of Chicago), my schooling, were to be allowed to determine the course of my life. I did not intend to be wholly dependent on history and culture. Full dependency must mean that I was done for. The commonest teaching of the civilised world in our time can be stated simply: 'Tell me where you come from and I will tell you what you are'.[6]

On this view, education can enable students to understand themselves by facilitating the development of autonomy and the critical assessment of social and cultural circumstances. It is a view which has great currency in modern philosophy of education, but it is not obviously conducive to solving problems of education in multicultural societies because it renders problematic our attitude to those groups and cultural communities which do not themselves value autonomy. Thus, for example, Joseph Raz urges that 'in an autonomy-supporting environment there is no choice but to be autonomous' and therefore members of such minority cultures must be brought 'humanely and decently' to placing value on the condition of autonomy.[7] Because autonomy is of great practical importance in democratic societies, non-autonomy valuing groups will not flourish unless they cultivate it. The development of autonomy is therefore not so much a moral as a practical necessity which must, if needs be, over-ride considerations of cultural loyalty. So this interpretation of 'understanding ourselves' is one which threatens to drive out cultural loyalties, particularly loyalties to cultures which give priority to virtues such as obedience or humility rather than self-determination or autonomy. Certainly this seems to be the slightly uneasy conclusion of Raz's argument, and it also, I think, lies behind Miller's suspicion of multicultural education, since it provides a definite context within which the claims of cultural loyalty and the claims of citizen identity will conflict.

There are, however, two other ways of interpreting the claim that education should enable us to understand ourselves. One, which is emphasised by Susan Wolf in her commentary on Taylor, is that education should enable us to understand and reflect upon our cultural heritage. She writes: 'we may think of education not merely as a way of acquainting students with what is best, but also as learning to understand *ourselves, our* history, *our* environment, *our* language'.[8] And she goes on to argue for the inclusion of African, Asian, Latin American and East European story books in public libraries; this, she says, has enabled Americans to see themselves as essentially multicultural. 'The most significant good is not that our stock of legends is now better or more comprehensive than before. It is, rather, that by having these books and by reading them, we come to recognize ourselves as a multicultural community and so to recognize and respect the members of that community in all *our* diversity'.[9]

I do not wish to take issue either with the sentiment or with the strategy which lies behind this conclusion. It does seem to me, however, to be a strategy which is available only on certain assumptions, most notably on the assumption that the stories from other lands really do tell us something about *ourselves*. In the United States, which is through its history essentially multicultural, this may be a plausible account, but it is far less readily conceded in Britain, where the disputed issue is precisely whether it is true that these 'other' cultures are in any way part of 'us', or we part of them. One commentator has suggested, that 'this polyphony of voices, this constant eddying of claims to identity, is one of the things that makes America America',[10] but for better or worse it is implausible to say the same about Britain, or about many other multicultural societies.

However, what I want to concentrate on here is a slightly different, though connected, implication of Wolf's account. By emphasising the importance of all these different stories to *our* community, she implies that there is, in the end, no significant distinction between the cultural heritage of African-Americans, Italian-Americans, Irish-Americans and so on. American identity transcends and includes all these different and diverse origins. Understanding ourselves therefore involves understanding all these different and diverse backgrounds — understanding them as all and equally *ours*. In this, I think, there may be both mistake and loss. The mistake lies in supposing that all such identities are correctly represented as 'hyphenated', but as Amy Gutmann has pointed out 'because of the systematic social injustice against African-Americans that persists over time, the identity of a significant proportion of African-Americans is not comfortably hyphenated (as the name African-American might suggest) but rather conflictually divided (African versus American) . . . without this added sense of suffering from systematic injustice, African-American identity would be similar in form (but not in content) to that of Irish-Americans, Korean-Americans, Jewish-Americans, and many other hyphenated-American identities'.[11] The mistake therefore is to suppose that each hyphenated group bears the same relation to the transcendent community of Americans. It is to suppose that the members of these groups feel no pressure to choose between the different component parts of their identity. And in some cases that assumption is false.

However, in addition to this mistake, there is also, I believe, the potential for loss inherent in the very desire to render all identities hyphenated in the way Wolf proposes, and I shall now attempt to say why I think there is loss and how a third interpretation of 'understanding ourselves' might serve to minimise that loss.

My third interpretation takes its cue from a recent book by Bernard Williams. In *Shame and Necessity* Williams asks why we should study the texts of the ancient Greeks, and he answers that we should do so at least partly in order to understand ourselves. However, for Williams, 'understanding ourselves' does not simply mean 'understanding our cultural heritage' (seeing where we have come from), nor does it mean 'developing autonomy' (critically evaluating where we have come from). It also means seeing ourselves *as autonomy valuers* and recognising the merits and defects of that position by comparison with others. Thus he writes: 'when the ancients speak, they do not merely tell us about themselves. They tell us about us. They do that in every case in which they can be made to speak, because they tell us who we are. That is, of course, the most general point of our attempts to make them speak. They can tell us not just who we are, but who we are not: they can denounce the falsity or the partiality or the limitations of our images of ourselves'.[12] It is, I think, for this reason that we should reject both Wolf's attempt to make 'our' culture include all other cultures, and Raz's attempt to make other cultures subservient to our culture. The pretence that our culture includes all others is just that — a pretence; and, as Gutmann points out, a damaging one in some cases. On the other hand, the insistence on the practical priority of our culture is, somewhat paradoxically, uncritical about the importance we attach to critical evaluation.

I shall try to elucidate this last claim by appeal to two examples, one taken from Williams himself, the other from Norvin Richards' discussion of humility. In the chapter of his book titled 'Shame and autonomy' Williams draws attention to the ancient Greek concept of shame and its relationship to the modern concept of guilt. It is often argued that the ancient Greeks had a shame culture whereas we have a guilt culture, and this distinction is also obliquely referred to by Taylor when he notes the move in modernity from an ethic of honour to an ethic of dignity. Indeed, in Taylor's eyes it is precisely this move which generates the problem of recognition that lies at the centre of his discussion:

> in those earlier societies, what we would now call identity was largely fixed by one's social position . . . the birth of a democratic society doesn't by itself do away with this phenomenon, because people can still define themselves by their social roles. What does decisively undermine this socially derived identification, however, is the ideal of authenticity itself. As this emerges, for instance, with Herder, it calls on me to discover my own original way of being. By definition, this way cannot be socially derived, but must be inwardly generated.[13]

The crucial move which Taylor alludes to here is the move from a culture in which identity is determined from without to a culture — a democratic culture — in which identity is determined (or is thought to be determined) from within the individual. The rejection of social determination was a natural concomitant of the decline of hierarchy, but with it came a wholly implausible view of the possibility of dispensing entirely with recognition by 'significant others' as an important component in the construction of identity. Thus, by placing too much emphasis on ourselves as self-evaluators, we run the risk of ignoring the extent to which even 'we moderns' require recognition by others: 'we define our identity always in dialogue with, sometimes in struggle against, the things our significant others want to see in us. Even after we outgrow some of these others — our parents, for instance — and they disappear from our lives, the conversation with them continues within us as long as we live'.[14]

Similarly, in Williams' account, the distinction between the ancient Greek understanding and our own is that the Greeks gave centrality to shame, understood as a feeling about ourselves generated by others' views of us, whereas we give centrality to guilt, understood as an inward recognition of what it is that we have done. Thus Williams notes that shame is often explicated by analogies of sight, and particularly by analogies of nakedness in the eyes of others. To experience shame is to be seen by others in a certain way, and (crucially) to know that one is the way they perceive one as being. In Sophocles' play, Ajax asks:

What countenance can I show my father Telamon?
How will he bear the sight of me
If I come before him naked, without any glory,
When he himself had a great crown of men's praise?
It is not something to be borne.

It is tempting, as Williams notes, to interpret the emphasis on shame as indicative of a culture which lacks any understanding of the moral in a Kantian sense. The heroes of Greek tragedy appear to be concerned not with what they have done, but with how they are perceived. They live not in their own estimation of themselves, but in the eyes of others. And this, of course, is quite contrary to modern (specifically Kantian) morality: 'in the Kantian scheme of oppositions, shame is on the bad side of all the lines'.[15] However, to dismiss shame as an ignoble concern with and dependence upon the views of others is misleading both with respect to the Greeks and with respect to ourselves. It is misleading with respect to ourselves because, as Taylor points out, we cannot both reject shame and yet acknowledge that 'a person or group of people can suffer real damage, real distortion, if the people or society around them mirror back to them a confining or demeaning or contemptible picture of themselves'.[16] We do still, and always, live partly in the eyes of others and even if their picture of us is distorted or unfair, it may still be a picture which influences our own views of who we are. In this sense, the concept of shame is not entirely alien to us.

Nevertheless, shame is less central to modern conceptions of morality than it was for the ancient Greeks. But this difference also may enable us the better to understand ourselves and the limitations of our moral world. If, following Williams, we take guilt to be centrally concerned with what we have done, and shame to be centrally concerned with what we are, then the modern emphasis on guilt leads in the direction of making reparation to those who have been wronged, but it does not, in itself, lead in the direction of rebuilding oneself.[17] By making guilt central, therefore, we foreclose on the kind of moral understanding which demands a reconstruction of ourselves in the light of others' opinions of us. And this is not, or not always, indicative of a noble refusal to live in the reflection of others' opinions. It is also symptomatic of an inability to move beyond an acknowledgement of what we have done to an acknowledgement of what we should be. Here, then, is a second sense in which other cultures — this time the culture of the ancient Greeks — may enable us the better to understand ourselves. If Williams' analysis is correct, the ancient Greeks suggest to us that we are the kinds of people who will make recompense for what we have done, but not the kind of people who will be capable of rebuilding ourselves. And the reason for that is precisely because we emphasise the solitary notion of guilt to the near exclusion of the more relational concept of shame.

What I am suggesting here is that understanding ourselves is a central aim of education, but 'understanding ourselves' may have various interpretations. It may mean understanding our cultural heritage, understanding 'where we have come from', but in that case it is a problematic injunction in cases where the disputed issue is precisely whether members of minority cultures are part of 'us' — whether their identity is hyphenated rather than divided. Alternatively, it may mean developing our autonomy, understanding what are the important values for us as individuals living in a democratic society, but that threatens intolerance and repression of those who are not autonomy-valuing. Finally, it may mean understanding ourselves *as autonomy valuers*, recognising that our values are the values of modern, democratic societies. As such, they may simultaneously be both more and less contiguous with the values of other cultures than we are inclined to imagine.

To illustrate this point further, I shall introduce a second example, taken from Norvin Richards' book, *Humility*. Richards asks: how can humility count as a virtue in modern Western society? And he answers that it can so count if we understand it not as 'holding oneself in low esteem', but rather as 'having oneself in proper perspective'. The humble person is not someone who puts a low value on his own talents. Rather, he is someone who makes a proper assessment of those talents. Moreover, this account of humility is one which, according to Richards, can transcend considerations of time and place: members of other cultures may value themselves more harshly than we do, but they can all concur in the analysis of humility as understanding oneself aright. Richards, then, is inclined to see our culture as transcending and including other cultures. When we study those other cultures, we will see that they are at root very much like ours. And in order to substantiate his claim he draws attention to the Old Order Amish and their renunciation of personal ambition as inconsistent with proper humility. Richards argues that ambition need not be inconsistent with humility either for the Amish or for us, since humility (properly understood) requires only that we not take *undue* pride in what we achieve. It does not require the rejection of personal achievement or ambition.

I give this example because it seems to me to ignore the important sense in which enlarging the canon, or studying other cultures, may enable us to understand ourselves. In Amish culture, at least as it is portrayed in the literature, what is most important is to be forgetful of oneself, to give oneself up to the community, or to 'disappear rather than stand out'. As one writer puts it: 'the size and number of mirrors in a society indicate the cultural importance attached to the self. Thus it is not surprising that the mirrors found in Amish houses are smaller and fewer than those found in modern ones'.[18] What this suggests to me is not that both we and the Amish share a concept of humility as 'having oneself in proper perspective'. What it suggests is that for the Amish, but not for us, any concern for 'proper perspective' is itself a threat to humility. Interpreting humility as 'understanding oneself aright' can be acceptable only to people who think that understanding oneself aright is a legitimate and important aim. But it is at least arguable that the Amish do not think that and therefore, for them, humility has both a different meaning and a different significance. They would interpret the very desire to 'understand oneself aright' as a desire which sprang from an inappropriate, indeed morally reprehensible, concern with oneself and one's own moral standing.[19]

What we learn from this is indeed something about ourselves: we learn that we are the kind of people for whom self-assessment is morally legitimate. But we also learn that this is something which makes humility a different and more difficult concept for us than it is for the Amish, since we are required to provide an interpretation of humility according to which it is both virtuous and consists in a concern with oneself which borders on the narcissistic. We learn that the price of self-assessment is the loss, or at least the deformation, of humility as it was originally conceived. We learn, in Williams' words, 'the falsity or the partiality or the limitations of our images of ourselves'.

CONCLUSION

I have suggested that the fundamental aim of education is to enable students to understand themselves. But this does not mean simply that they should recognise their own cultural heritage, nor yet that they should form their own opinions by critical reflection on that cultural heritage. It also, and crucially, means that they should understand themselves as the kinds of people for whom critical reflection, autonomy and self-fulfilment are central. This, I have argued, is the way in which education can enable us, particularly those of us who belong to the dominant groups in democratic societies, to understand ourselves.

How does this understanding of the aim of education help to answer the question with which I began, namely 'how can we educate people in a way which both respects their cultural identity and fits them for citizenship in a democratic society?' It does so in two ways: first, if we enlarge the canon and deploy it as a means of increasing self-understanding among the majority as well as the minority, one result may be that the majority will revise their own estimation of themselves. To revert to the example used earlier, by understanding Amish values I may come to see my own interest in self-fulfilment as partial, or even as partly misplaced. I may be more willing, not merely to acknowledge other values, but also to see the constraints of my own value system. If this happens, then the contest between citizen identity and cultural loyalty will become less acute, since cultural loyalty will both inform and transform citizen identity.

In my opening remarks, I referred to David Miller's insistence that 'political education must try to shape cultural identities in the direction of common citizenship. It must try to present an interpretation of Indian culture in Britain which makes it possible for members of the Indian community to feel at home in, and loyal to the British state. In so far as there are elements in Indian culture which are at odds with such a reconciliation, the interpretation must be selective or, if you like, biased'. But this seems to require that the interpretation of Indian culture should be malleable, whereas the interpretation of British citizenship remains fixed. I see no reason, however, why the concept of British citizenship should not also be malleable. Not, of course, in Wolf's sense that being British or being American transcends and includes all these different cultural loyalties, but certainly in the sense that we (the majority) may come to recognise things of value in those other cultures and attempt to incorporate, or at least acknowledge, some of them in our societies and in the construction of our sense of citizenship.

Secondly, and connectedly, by enlarging the canon we may come to see that some problems which are presented as problems of toleration are in fact problems of recognition. Reflecting on the invitation to relativism inherent in his presumption of equal worth, Taylor writes: 'it makes sense to demand as a matter of right that we approach the study of certain cultures with a presumption of their value . . . but it can't make sense to demand as a matter of divine right that we come up with a final concluding judgement that their value is great or equal to others'.[20] But this too invites a false choice: either other cultures are better than ours, or they are worse — or we must submit to cultural relativism. The discussion of the Amish and Williams' discussion of the ancient Greeks suggest, however, that there are at least some cases where this simple division does not do justice to the situation. We have gained autonomy; they have retained humility, and there may be no answer to Taylor's question: 'is their value equal to or greater than ours?' Moreover, to say this is not to submit to a crude cultural relativism. It is merely to suggest that the question is the wrong one to pose. As autonomy-valuers we are prone to identify the oppressive nature of Amish culture, and we may decide to tolerate that oppressiveness. But if we employ education as a means of understanding ourselves, we may also come to see that as autonomy-valuers we lack the moral language with which to provide an explanation of their humility as anything other than oppression. In this way, we learn something about the limitations of our own moral world. We learn that there are virtues which are valuable, yet which cannot properly be accommodated within a moral framework which gives centrality to self-assessment and autonomy.

I began with the question 'how can we educate people in a way which both respects their cultural identity and instils democratic values in them?' My partial and tentative answer is that we should *not* begin by trying to understand, include or tolerate members of minority groups. Rather, we should begin by trying to understand ourselves and, if it is not too paradoxical, to understand ourselves as the kind of people who may place altogether too much importance on self-understanding.

ACKNOWLEDGEMENTS

This paper was written for the International Conference on Education for Democracy which was held in Jerusalem, June 1993. It was also delivered at the Philosophy of Education conference in Gregynog, July 1994. I am grateful to the participants at both conferences for their helpful comments, and especially to Yael Tamir and Paul Standish for extending the invitations to me.

NOTES AND REFERENCES

1. Miller, D., *Market, State and Community: Theoretical Foundations of Market Socialism*, Oxford: Clarendon Press, 1989, p. 291.

2. Taylor, C., The politics of recognition, in: A. Gutmann (ed.) *Multiculturalism and the Politics of Recognition*, Princeton: Princeton University Press, 1992, p. 66.
3. *Ibid.*, p. 71.
4. *Ibid.*, p. 65.
5. *Ibid.*, pp. 66ff.
6. Bloom, A., *The Closing of the American Mind*, Harmondsworth: Penguin Books, 1987, p. 13.
7. Raz, J., *The Morality of Freedom*, Oxford: Oxford University Press, 1986, p. 301.
8. Taylor, *op. cit.*, p. 84.
9. *Ibid.*, p. 83.
10. Hughes, R., *Culture of Complaint*, New York: Oxford University Press, 1993, p. 95.
11. Gutmann, A., The challenge of multiculturalism in political ethics, *Philosophy and Public Affairs*, 1993, p. 186.
12. Williams, B., *Shame and Necessity*, University of California Press, 1993, p. 20.
13. Taylor, *op. cit.*, pp. 31–32.
14. *Ibid.*, pp. 32–33.
15. Williams, *op. cit.*, p. 77.
16. Taylor, *op. cit.*, p. 25.
17. Williams, *op. cit.*, p. 94.
18. Richards, N., *Humility*, Philadelphia: Temple University Press, 1992, p. 181.
19. It has been suggested to me that the example of the Amish is problematic in two ways: first, because Amish culture is less self-effacing than is often supposed in the literature, or at least that it lacks the homogeneity which is usually attributed to it. I owe this point to Amy Gutmann and it is persuasively argued, though in a slightly different context, in her article 'The challenge of multiculturalism in political ethics', *Philosophy and Public Affairs*, 1993, pp. 171–206. Secondly, and connectedly, Paul Standish has suggested to me that the people who genuinely embrace the values I refer to here will be anonymous and unsung heroes, not the sorts of people about whom a large body of literature has been written. These are important considerations, but I hope that my general point survives the specific difficulties.
20. Taylor, *op. cit.*, pp. 68–9.

Liberalism and the Aims of
Multicultural Education[1]

WALTER FEINBERG

I. LIBERAL CONCEPTIONS OF SELF, CULTURE AND OPPORTUNITY

Most Americans, whatever their political affiliation, have been strongly influenced by philosophical liberalism, or the ideals about individuality, independence and autonomy developed by philosophers such as Locke, Jefferson, Mill and Rawls. This influence extends to our conception of educational aims as we emphasise the importance of individual development and choice, and it extends to our understanding of educational research where the more prominent paradigms take as the primary unit of analysis individual differences in such things as motivation, intelligence or environment.

Recent feminist and postmodern critics of liberalism have accused it of being too individualistic and insensitive to the socially constituted character of the self. Liberal educators have also been criticised for ignoring the special character and needs of minority cultures. Often this criticism accuses educators of failing to acknowledge the contributions of non-European groups to American civilisation and to the civilisation of the world. When it takes this form such criticism may or may not be empirically correct, but it is not in fact a telling criticism of traditional philosophical liberalism.

There is nothing in liberal doctrine *per se* that would prohibit it from teaching about the contribution of different cultures to our collective heritage, and many programmes are available to teach children about other cultures. Liberalism requires neutrality with regard to ideas of the good life, but it does not require ignorance with regard to different conceptions of the good life. In this sense liberalism is no enemy to multicultural education, and some of the recent criticisms of the liberal agenda have been misdirected. Questions of balance and proportion may well be raised but there is little in liberal theory itself that would lead one to reject learning about other cultures.

However, there is an element of multicultural education which liberal theorists would have problems accepting: it is what I call learning-through-culture. In short it is the view of education premised on the idea that children do not appropriate the world directly, as if, in Locke's terms, they were a *tabula rasa* waiting to be impacted by sensations caused by outside forces. Instead the idea that we learn-through-culture affirms the view that the structures of meaning and significance into which we are born, together with the symbol and socialisation systems that enable us to decode and participate in these structures, establish distinctive ways of relating to one another, of appropriating information and of establishing goals. Given these distinct ways of appropriating meaning, it is important for educators to attend to these differences — both as objects of educational research and as an agenda for educational practice.

In this paper I argue that there is an important, although neglected, distinction in multicultural education between learning about a culture and learning-through-culture. I also argue that liberalism has no problem on a philosophical level with the first of these as an educational goal, but that the second does present problems. However, I argue that these are not insurmountable. I also argue that once we understand the vital role played by culture then educational research will need to focus significant attention on the cultural resources through which learning occurs. This means that researchers will need to understand the styles, horizons and goals through which children from different cultural groups approach education. In arguing for this view of learning as culturally implicated, it should not be thought that I am suggesting that culture is a closed, impervious shield that shuts a student off from the work and insights of others. Culture is a window, not a cell. However, there are instances where a fragile culture may well need special protection from unintended assaults from more dominant groups.

In this paper I want to present reasons for expanding our traditional understanding of the liberal heritage to provide a wider scope for cultural difference. I argue that while certain interpretations of liberalism may have difficulty with the idea that learning takes place through culture, liberalism as a philosophical movement has sufficient intellectual resources actually to accept this insight and contribute to its development. I will suggest as well that once liberalism begins to accommodate these insights it can add important dimensions to the educational research agenda.

One word of caution. The paper is meant neither as a full-blown defence of liberalism nor as a full-blown critique. The point that I want to make — that liberalism has the intellectual resources to account for learning-through-culture — is important precisely because we need to understand the resources that are contained in this, our most influential social theory. To demonstrate that liberalism has more resources than is commonly thought is not to say that it has all the resources that education in our modern society requires. However, this is a different issue and needs a wider analysis that would include an examination of the economic and political institutions that have come, correctly or incorrectly, to be associated with the liberal state.

The kind of learning that I have in mind when I speak of learning-through-culture is reflected in the research of, say, Shirley Brice Heath on literacy and in her view that children from different cultures have different ways with words that must be respected as school literacy is established. It is reflected in a different way in the pedagogy of Paulo Freire and others who suggest that different cultures may have different educational ends-in-view. Hence culture provides both the means of learning and the tentative end. Nevertheless it is important to keep in mind that the existence or non-existence of significant cultural variation is a matter to be determined by careful observation and empirical research, not by dogmatic affirmations of unique identity.

Liberalism in its modern form emphasises individual development and growth. It should not have difficulty accommodating the idea of multicultural education where that ideal indicates that one learns about other cultures from the perspective of a dominant, central culture. It does, however, have more difficulty accommodating the ideal of cultural diversity where diversity means that difference will be celebrated in a way that enables children to learn through their own cultural practices.

One reason for this is in part the fear that if children learn through their own cultural forms — where that culture differs from the mainstream — they will be cut off from many economic, political and social opportunities. Yet children who are cut off from their cultural heritage may also experience alienation and rootlessness, and the jury is still out on the question of the economic benefits of emphasising cultural uniformity at the expense of diversity. The deeper and more important reason for this difficulty is liberalism's commitment to the individual as the unit of both theoretical analysis and moral authority, and it is this aspect of the difficulty that I want to address.

The difficulty does not arise just because liberalism places higher priority on economic opportunity than it does on cultural expression, although many argue that students must be skilled in the ways of the dominant culture if they are to take advantage of the economic and professional opportunities offered by the larger society.

There is nothing in the doctrine of liberalism that would disallow a person from choosing a certain form of cultural expression even if in doing so he or she implicitly loses certain economic and professional opportunities. Rather the difficulty for liberalism is two-fold. First it arises because of the emphasis that traditional liberal theory places on individual choice and because of the view that in privileging certain kinds of cultural beliefs and practices too early, the child's capacity for choice is curtailed. The second reason is political and involves the belief that social harmony, if not solidarity, depends upon a level of cultural uniformity in the public realm. In this paper I want to focus on the first of these concerns, but I will say a few words in the conclusion about the second.

My strategy in this paper will be to show that in its emphasis on individual choice liberal theorists make a mistake if they underestimate the extent to which culture is implicated in choice and provides its foundation. I illustrate the paralysis that can result by underestimating the importance of culture through a classroom example involving two Japanese children in an American school. I then analyse the kind of cultural learning which breaks the paralysis and, in doing so, I make a critical distinction between cultural competence and cultural understanding as educational aims. The point of the example is to suggest that, given liberalism's concern for enhancing individual choice, it must be able to recognise the culturally implicated nature of learning for different groups of children. Once the relationship between culture and choice is developed, then we are in a position to reformulate the goals of multicultural education. Through this strategy I am also trying to show that acknowledgement of cultural diversity is not, at its deepest level, incompatible with the commitments of liberalism, and I suggest that cultural understanding involves more than learning about another culture. It also involves using that learning in a reflexive way to understand one's own behaviour and practices as a culturally constructed product. A form of educational research that seeks to reconstruct these cultural products and to establish them as objects of discourse can establish the foundation for productive forms of inter-cultural relations.

II. TEACHING ABOUT AND TEACHING-THROUGH-CULTURE: THE STANDARD LIBERAL CONCERN

While liberalism has little difficulty in teaching children about other cultures, it often experiences problems in enabling children to learn through a culture other than the dominant one. It is believed that learning about different cultures brings people together without diminishing the individual's capacity to choose a life style of his or her own later as an adult. What I call learning through an alternative culture — say the culture of one's parents — provides a different problem. Learning-through-culture entails not just learning to recognise the tastes and behaviours of a cultural minority. It involves adopting the norms, standards and general ways of being of that group. For children from minority cultures this learning may involve different standards and different goals, and in some instances it may curtail the child's future ability to choose from the array of alternatives provided by the larger social order. This is one of the strongest arguments against allowing fundamentalist parents to remove their children from the classroom when certain objectionable passages are taught in the school text. The argument is not just that such passages often represent the latest scientific or scholarly thinking on a subject — after all there are many areas in which most of us get away with dated or even misguided understanding. It is that failure to understand such matters limits a child's choice and hinders the likelihood that he or she will be able intelligently to choose between different alternatives. This is also the concern behind the dissent in the Yoder case,[2] and it is frequently the reason for liberal objections to the kind of bilingual education that serves to celebrate and maintain a local culture rather than simply bridging the gap between the local community and the larger economic and political structure.

It is important that we understand the specific nature of the objection as consistent with traditional liberal democratic theory. The objection is not that children will have fewer opportunities if the parents are allowed to reject the curriculum, although this is certainly a concern. The theoretical objection is that the children will not develop the capacity to choose whether or not they want to take advantage of those opportunities. It is not that the child will therefore end up repeating the life practices of the parent, but rather that the child will have no other choice but to do this. In other words, liberal theory rejects these practices in the school not because it privileges opportunity over community, but because it privileges individual choice over both of these.

Indeed, the ideal of community — of people working together to accomplish a common end ready to serve individual members in time of need — is as much a part of American liberalism as is individual opportunity and is memorialised in images of town meetings, community barn-raising and immigrant self-help groups. These images represent a central feature of the American ideal and an acceptable consequence of liberal individualism: one where individuals voluntarily come together for mutual aid and enrichment. However, the important point is that these are *voluntary* communities constituted through the choice of individuals. The reason certain liberals have difficulty with multiculturalism is that they see people first as individuals and that they believe that people, as individuals, then create communities.

Yet precisely because we are first and foremost individuals who may choose or not choose to be members of communities it is thought that we should suffer no disapprobation should we choose not to engage with others in a communal context. As long as we pay our taxes and obey the law we are meeting our obligations. This is the minimal notion of citizenship, but as the minimal notion it is also a sufficient one—anything more, liberal theory holds, is intrusive and in danger of violating individual rights. The consistent liberal objects, therefore, as much to government as to cultural intrusion on individual choice. On this view the role of education is thereby to facilitate, not to direct, choice.

III. PROBLEMS WITH THE STANDARD CONCEPTION OF SELF AND COMMUNITY

There are a number of problems with the conceptions of self and community that are reflected in the recent debate on educational reform, a debate which largely fails to consider the role of cultural factors in learning. First, in contrast to the image of the self conveyed in traditional liberal writings, we are in fact born into social configurations and our choices are reflections of those configurations. We choose as members of cultural groups, not as isolated, dispassionate individuals, and my membership already influences the kind of alternatives I accept as true choices. To say that I choose as an individual is to forget just how much culture is implicated in my individual choice.

A second problem involves the recent failure of traditional liberalism to provide the intellectual foundation for a conception of cultural freedom. Traditional liberalism was intended to liberate individuals from the economic and political constraints of established authority. One of the insights of postmodern theory is the recognition that traditional individualism has little to say about the need for cultural expression and serves, perhaps inadvertently, to support institutions which repress lifestyles that are out of step with the tendency towards more collective and corporate forms of economic organization. One of the reasons people fight so hard against assaults on their communal standards is precisely that community stands as the bearer of culture, and culture is that which provides meaning and significance to the choices people make. Hence to reject one culture in order to establish another is, as Will Kymlicka suggests, to reject the very foundation on which choice is made.[3]

A third problem with traditional liberalism is that it treats the self as basically fixed and essentially ineducable with regard to its own nature. In the classical utilitarian formulation, individual wants are reduced to the desire to seek pleasure and avoid pain; and in the behaviourist's reformulation all individuals can be motivated through the manipulation of appropriate external stimuli. What an individual wants, however, is essentially unconnected with what that individual is. All individuals are seen as essentially the same: they seek to maximise satisfaction or, in some theories, to minimise dissatisfaction. Self-understanding is largely restricted to knowing what kinds of objects will achieve this end[4] and whether one has the drive, ability and desire needed to acquire these objects. This view reflects the doctrine of the fixed self which assumes that individuality is essentially independent of community and is reflected in the most prominent proposals to correct our educational crisis. In most of these proposals individual choice is paramount and cultural expression, if mentioned at all, is relegated to a minor concern.

For example, one group of reformers sees the state as simply a mechanism for distributing educational resources leaving to individual parents alone the choice of where their children should go to school and what they should be taught. Other reformers emphasise the potential economic benefits of schooling both to individual students and to the nation, and propose a curriculum that would improve students' ability to support themselves and to contribute to the nation's economic well-being. Those who advocate this view want to narrow the offerings of the school, eliminate the so-called frill subjects, increase the number of required subjects and require the same subjects in every school. They want to make schools across the country increasingly similar to one another in terms of curriculum content and they want this content to have a cash value. Those who emphasise the economic benefits of schools do not see any conflict between their view, which calls for constricting the offerings of the curriculum, and the view that advocates the widest possible choice for parents. This is because they assume that all parents and all cultures hold economic success as their major educational goal, that they all share the same meaning of such success — the private accumulation of wealth.[5] Thus they advocate providing parents with more choice as they seek to reduce the variety of alternatives from which parents might choose. A third response is to accept the role of education as a public-forming body but to emphasise meanings and symbols that are thought to be shared and culturally neutral. In all these proposals schools are intended to empower individuals and culture is largely incidental to this process.

There are two questions to be asked at this point: the first is whether culture really can be incidental to the empowerment of individuals. The issue is extremely complicated, but in general I accept the view that because culture is that through which we learn we cannot be empowered outside culture. Yet it would be wrong to suggest that learning must forever be restricted to a single cultural form. Cultures can both grow together and grow apart. Nor should it be taken to mean that no communication between cultures is possible and that children cannot appropriate material from one culture to the next without suffering a disadvantage. This is clearly empirically false in many instances, and in those cases where it is not false it should be viewed as posing serious problems, not as offering a general principle of learning. The second question is whether empowerment must always be empowerment of the individual as such and whether culture, like schooling, must be treated as simply instrumental to this end. This question is even more complex than the first, and requires a separate paper. However, I would suggest, with Kymlicka,[6] that in certain, although limited, cases where individual desire and cultural well-being conflict, there are reasonable arguments for choosing to strengthen culture. I believe that this was the direction in which the majority of the court was going in the Yoder case although its rationale was not spelled out quite in these terms.

IV. THE GOALS OF A DEMOCRATIC, MULTICULTURAL EDUCATION[7]

Ultimately what is involved in multicultural education is much the same as what is involved in the development of a democratic public. We are learning how to listen and how to discourse about our differences where the rules of discourse — both our own and others' rules — are part of what we are listening for. Yet different groups need not listen to the same things. Although both dominant and subordinate groups require to learn about the ways of different cultures, they do not always need to learn exactly the same things. Consider the different lessons that are being learned in the example below by the Japanese and the American children in the first grade classroom.

A new group of Japanese children have just arrived with their parents in Cornton, a middle-sized American city. Their fathers have been sent to the community as managers and engineers to set up a large factory which will employ a workforce of thousands. Two of these children were assigned to Mrs. Fields' first grade class and much of Mrs. Fields' time was spent helping the two new Japanese first graders feel comfortable in their new school. She deliberately sat the Japanese children next to students who were bright, friendly and popular to ensure that the children would have someone to play with. During the early weeks of school, Sara, who sat next to Kayoko, was placed in Kayoko's low reading group, even though her ability would have placed her in the advanced group. The arrangement seemed to be acceptable to Sara's parents who said they thought it was a good experience for her and it helped Kayoko to feel comfortable.

The Japanese children were seated so that they could communicate with their American partners and with each other if they chose to do so. The children were usually seated in rows. Each row had two desks grouped together. Hence while Takeo and Kayoko were each paired with an American child, they sat next to each other with an aisle separating them.

For the first few weeks Takeo and Kayoko never spoke to each other, even in Japanese. Although Mrs. Fields reported that Sara and Kayoko communicated with a combination of gestures, smiles, nods, 'almost by magic', English words were not available to either Takeo or Kayoko, and neither was willing to break the ice and communicate in Japanese. They were linguistically paralysed at this point. The language they could speak was no longer perceived by them as legitimate for this classroom while the language that had legitimacy in the school was unavailable to them.

This silence was disturbing to Mrs. Fields. While she was pleased to see Kayoko and Sara communicating with each other by whatever 'magic' they used, she wondered about the adequacy of her own efforts to encourage the Japanese students to speak, and she reported with delight the process that had finally broken their mutual silence.

Paula came up to me this afternoon to complain that Takeo had said something to her in Japanese and she didn't know what he said, but she didn't think it sounded 'nice'. She said it sounded like 'swat'. Paula wanted me to ask Takeo what he said. I thought he had probably told her to sit down and I said 'suwatte' and he nodded yes. Then to practise my Japanese I said 'tatte' and he stood up and nodded that was correct. Paula watched this fascinated and then commented that Takeo and I had understood one another and that I could speak Japanese. She then asked me to teach her too.

Then others in the room said that they wanted to know Japanese so that they could talk to Takeo and Kayoko. Sara said that her sister even knew a word in Japanese and why wouldn't I teach them. I had wanted to wait awhile... but I decided that I had the 'teachable' moment right then. We stopped what we were doing and I taught 'Konnichi-wa' and 'dewa mata'. The American kids were... all raising their hands wanting to respond.

Prior to this episode the Japanese children had been reluctant to respond when Mrs. Fields attempted to address them in her limited Japanese and Mrs. Fields had never observed them speaking to each other in her classroom. The day after Paula's complaint things had changed.

What a day. My aide and I had Takeo teaching us to say the parts of the face in Japanese. Then I checked his and Kayoko's math papers, counting in Japanese (to practise my Japanese). After that the whole class practised saying 'good afternoon', 'see you later', and 'good evening' in Japanese... A little later Sara came up to tell me to come back and listen to Takeo and Kayoko talking in Japanese. This was a first! There they were chattering away in Japanese and not paying one bit of attention. This was the first time I had heard them speak to one another.

Mrs. Fields' teaching reveals a model for multicultural education. It suggests that the expression of alternative identities should be encouraged but not forced by the teacher. What makes the important difference in this case is her ability to engage the children on their own cultural and linguistic grounds, providing the security they need to enter the group as equals. This ability had been developed over time and required a passing familiarity with Japanese culture and a modest understanding of the Japanese language. She had only started to study Japanese a few months before this episode when she learned the children would be entering her class. The skill she had obtained in a few months was not enough to carry on a full conversation with the children, but it was sufficient to allow her to take advantage of 'the teachable moment' when it appeared.

These children have been introduced to an important feature of democratic and multicultural education. However, it is one that is considerably different from that imagined by the traditional philosophical liberal. It is an education in which culture is recognized as implicated in individual choice and empowerment. The children have been accepted into an established community with their own cultural identity resonably intact and they have been acknowledged for their ability to teach as well as to be taught. They have been allowed to make a difference in the community itself. Of course democratic education is a long-term affair requiring more than simply the acceptance of cultural difference. Mrs. Fields has made a start with these children, but her aim is not, I believe, to teach the Japanese children exactly the same lesson as the American children. In part she is teaching the former group that it is perfectly acceptable to be Japanese while also teaching them how to operate competently in American society. It is to be hoped that the American students are learning that their taken-for-granted behaviour is a cultural product and Mrs. Fields is teaching them an understanding of another culture's ways. While she may not voice it in these terms, she is indeed sensitive to the differences in status and power that these two groups occupy in this classroom.

Someone might observe, quite accurately, that the position of these children is only temporary and that in the long run the status of the Japanese children in the community would be at least as high as that of their classmates. The observation is important because of its suggestion that dominance and subordinance are complex concepts and that their application itself often requires a subtle discourse. Power is indeed multi-layered. However, the episode in Mrs. Fields' classroom is still significant for at least two reasons. First it demonstrates that power relations do need to be considered in determining what the aims of instruction should be in specific situations and, second, it highlights an important distinction in intercultural education — a distinction between competence and understanding.

All too often lower-status students are expected simply to become competent in the ways of the dominant group whereas no expectations are placed on students from the more advantaged situation. This is not the case in Mrs. Fields' classroom where there are mutual although different expectations. The Japanese students will become competent in many of the ways of American culture, but the American students will also achieve a certain level of understanding of Japanese culture.

Competence and understanding are related, but they are not the same. The American students will not be able to navigate Japanese culture while the Japanese students will soon learn how to cope in American society. They will come to be able to shop for their parents, and to converse with friends and teachers in English. They will come to know when they enter an American's home that they need not remove their shoes, and they will learn to be more assertive in the classroom. It is likely that they will acquire some understanding of American culture as well, but their competence level will not always parallel or even be related to their understanding level. The American students are not gaining a great deal of competence in terms of Japanese culture, but they are travelling on the track of understanding, however limited or extensive their trip may eventually be. Just what is entailed in this journey and what constitutes the kind of understanding that we have when we understand another culture?

V. COMPETENCE AND LEARNING-THROUGH-CULTURE

There is a distinction between having a native's competence and having an understanding of the culture. A native's competence enables us to navigate the culture — to know what to expect in response to certain behaviour and gestures, such as eye-contact or smiling. It also opens us up to the possibilities that are supplied to those who learn through the perspectives and categories provided by that culture. For example, as Shweder observes about moral learning in children:

> Moral interpretations of events are expressed through and are discernible in the very organization of routine practices (a separate bed for each child, a communal meal, lining up—first come, first served—to get tickets). In sum, it is our view that children's emerging moral understandings are the product of continuous participation in social practices (the mundane rituals of everyday life), and those socially produced and reproduced understandings are the grounding for later attempts reflexively or self-consciously to reconstruct their own moral code.[8]

Cultural competence is what we have when we are able to recognise and participate in the routines of another way of life and thereby guide a part of our own development by its conceptions of performance and excellence. The more competent we are the more smoothly we interact through gestures, expressions and everyday linguistic utterances, and the smoother these interactions the more open we are to learning through the cultural forms that they represent. To be fully competent therefore is to be able to learn through the developmental categories of the other much in the way a child learns, unmediated by previous understandings. This goal is, of course, impossible for adults, who have learned through alien cultural forms, fully to realize, for one always hear children's stories differently as an adult than as a child. Nevertheless, non-mediated learning-through-the other culture stands as an ideal of cultural competence. This is quite different from the ideal of cultural understanding.

VI. MEDIATION AND CULTURAL UNDERSTANDING

Whereas the goal of cultural competence is to enter the standpoint of the other as if this standpoint were unmediated by one's original way of life, cultural understanding is always undertaken with one's home culture in mind. Indeed, it is the initial sense of difference between home and other which raises the imperative of cultural understanding, and such understanding is undertaken with members of one's own cultural group as the implicit audience. In contrast to the striving for cultural competence, the goal of understanding is not to reach the point of learning through the other. Rather the categories through which learning occurs are important because, among other things, they can help to provide a critical sense of the possibilities and limitations that other ways of life make available. Thus one of the goals of cultural understanding is to make the culture-through-which-learning-occurs the object of discourse and analysis. Yet to do this requires that one's own cultural learning be raised, at some level, to an object of discourse and analysis. If this is not done, then the other is always in danger of being unconsciously reinterpreted and evaluated in our own terms and of being unintentionally distorted to conform to our own cultural categories. Obviously there are limitations to how much of one's own cultural forms can become objects for analysis at any one time since these are also the tools and the perspectives through which analysis is performed. Yet, by recognizing that learning occurs through culture, different components of cultural expression, religion, language, conceptions of time and space, etc. can be explored at different times using the cultural other as a point of comparison and relief.

VII. CULTURAL UNDERSTANDING AND MULTICULTURAL EDUCATION

Just as the process of understanding our own culture is complex, so too is the process of understanding other cultures; but it is not, as some theorists suggest, impossible, and it constitutes an essential element of democratic education in a multicultural society. Moreover, because the first step in such understanding involves viewing one's own activity and behaviour as a cultural product, understanding is usually more difficult for members of the dominant culture who are taught to take their own behaviour as modelling a cultural norm. Nevertheless, we do not, contrary to some recent arguments,[9] need to have a native's competence to understand the other. An understanding of the culture enables us to place this behaviour in a social and historical context. It helps us to understand just why it evokes the response it does. A person may have native competence without much understanding, as is the case with many intuitive people who know how to read the behaviour of others, but cannot say what the behaviour means or why it means what it does. Similarly a person may have a great deal of understanding without having any practised competence. Historians who have studied the customs and practices of an ancient people in significant detail have acquired much understanding but no competence.

It takes an awareness of another culture to have a conception of one's own behaviour as a cultural expression; this is the beginning of understanding. The native can tell us just what the eye movement means in her culture because she is aware of our culture and because she knows that different cultures interpret some behaviours differently. However, there is more to understanding than simply being able to say what a particular slice of behaviour means. For example, an anthropologist might tell us about some culture where looking a person in the eye is an indication of honesty because of the strong value that is placed on equality. The anthropologist might continue that dishonesty is thereby interpreted as a stain that will lower one's standing, making one less than equal, and people in this culture believe that this lowered standing will inevitably be expressed in one's posture and manner. The eyes are taken as the window to the soul and failing to look the other person in the eye is thereby taken as a sign of wrongdoing because it is seen to indicate the fear that if the window were open, the stain could be seen. The lie has literally reduced her standing in the eyes of others and in her own eyes as well. Here the interpretation given to the downward glance is an indication of a deeper set of beliefs about the nature of human beings and their relationship with one another. It is a sign of a well-formed set of beliefs that is imbedded within the practices of the culture. To say that a person understands a culture is to say that she has access to that set of beliefs and is able to reconstruct them when required.

This meaning of cultural understanding is the same whether the culture is our own or that of someone else, and it is not the same as learning to operate competently — even at the highest levels — in a culture. To be able to code a piece of behaviour — they show respect by glancing away — enables a person to navigate the culture. A person who is completely competent can navigate the culture intuitively, participate in its music, enjoy its stories and carry on many conversations. A person who is fully competent can participate in the culture from the inside. However, even this level of participation is distinguishable from understanding the culture.

When we understand another culture, we understand its core set of beliefs about self and other and we are able to translate these into particular patterns of behaviour. For example, where a glance to the side or to the floor is accepted as a sign of respect, it is likely to be an expression of a set of beliefs that is quite counter to the one that insists on 'looking the teacher in the eye'. Here looking the teacher in the eye may be a sign of disrespect because it presumes an equality which the culture requires be earned through the wisdom that comes from many years of experience. The essential relationship is one of inequality of experience and wisdom. The person who learns only to translate the behaviour — to take a glance at the floor as respect, not as dishonesty — has learned an important lesson, but nevertheless may be still quite ignorant about the culture. She knows how to show respect, but not why she is showing it or when it is appropriate to show it.

Behaviour is the gateway to participation. Meaning is the gateway to understanding. To progress no further than the level of proper behaviour is to lose an opportunity of using the practices of the other culture to learn something about the deeper meanings of our own. To develop this understanding requires an openness to the practices of the other culture without exclusively interpreting them through one's own immediate aims even though any fruitful dialogue will eventually involve bringing those aims back into focus. Nevertheless, one's own aims are often the reason for the dialogue to take place and their reassessment may well provide a reason for altering its nature. The way these American students come to see another culture such as Japan may eventually tell them something about the way they themselves are as Americans and may enable them better to evaluate their own possible futures. Here in the momentary decentring of their own culture is the core of cultural understanding. It is this act of decentring and of coming to terms with otherness that is perhaps the major task for the education of a democratic public in a multicultural society.

Both cultural competence and cultural understanding are important elements of multicultural education for all groups. However, because their behaviour is taken as the norm, understanding is more difficult and, therefore, more in need of systematic development, for members of the dominant group. One would hope that such understanding will be accompanied by certain positive attitudes, but no education can fully prescribe how one should feel about what one has come to understand. Education can at least further attitudes of patience and openness towards the other by advancing the reflective insight that contrasting groups are joined in the simple fact that their different norms and behaviours are historically and culturally constructed. And some forms of educational research can help teachers and administrators to understand the character of this construction and the various meanings it conveys.

VIII. THE CONTRAST BETWEEN THE LIBERAL MODEL OF INDIVIDUAL CHOICE AND THE CULTURALLY IMPLICATED MODEL

The twin aims of cultural competence and cultural understanding may be understood as a supplement to, rather than a rejection of, traditional philosophical liberalism. In this supplement the enhancement of individual choice still remains a paramount goal of education, but now the significance of cultural factors is given more recognition as an empowering factor enhancing individual autonomy. Yet the model of culturally implicated choice does move beyond traditional liberalism in so far as it seeks a form of self-understanding in which each of us comes to understand our own behaviour and norms as culturally constructed. Ultimately knowledge of the other culture enables the student to see her own position as contingent and subject to reflexive development and change. To be educated in a multicultural way means to understand the nature of this contingency and the possibilities for development and change that it provides. Hence regardless of one's cultural foundation there is something that all people who are educated in this way have in common: the recognition of a constructed contingent self whose understanding depends upon an acknowledgement of otherness. Here we move beyond the decultured self of liberalism and acknowledge a self that is always implicated in culture.

IX. SOCIAL HARMONY AND POLITICAL STABILITY

I have responded to the liberal's concern about multicultural education by suggesting that the acknowledgement of culture is implicated in individual choice and that, rather than limiting choice, a multicultural education, properly conceived, actually serves to enhance it. I have not, however, responded to all the very serious concerns that people have about this issue, and conclude by mentioning one that remains to be addressed — that of political and educational stability, and the belief among many traditional liberals that political stability requires a certain degree of cultural uniformity.

I have already indicated that this is a serious concern, but that the level of uniformity required by stability is a difficult and complicated question to address. It is, for example, likely to be the case that stability is furthered as much by ensuring the provision of reasonable health care and jobs as it is by advancing a uniform curriculum. While the jury is still out on this matter, I would agree up to a point with those who seek some common educational experience. To put the matter in metaphorical terms, even if the melting pot is replaced by a salad or a stew, we will still need a bowl or a crock-pot.

The more interesting question has to do with the obligation a society has to groups that are not much interested in having their children learn about other cultures and would also prefer that they not use such learning to gain a self-reflexive awareness of their own culturally constituted self. These are the groups which would want their children to leave the room when evolutionary theory is taught or which seek, through private education, to isolate their children from alternative ways of life. These issues are far too numerous and complex to handle here, but they merit a few words as to why the issue is problematic for liberal theory.

It is likely that in a multicultural society like our own an education that teaches children to view their own identities — their standards, norms and ways of life — as a cultural product is implicitly teaching them to respect people with other identities. In some ways each stands as an accident of history, but accident is the essence of historical life. Democracy that is informed by the character of cultural difference is the structure of political organisation that enables culturally constituted selves to thrive.

The problem represented by groups that seek to opt out of our multicultural education is best confronted by understanding its roots within our expanded liberal philosophy. On the one hand, liberalism tells us that we should not interfere with the choices of individuals and hence, by implication, it suggests that parents should have a large say regarding the character of the education of their children. On the other hand, the expanded, culturally implicated notion of choice that I have developed here suggests that liberalism and democracy themselves work best when people understand their own culturally constructed nature. Yet respect and cultural integration do not always go together, nor do cultural isolation and disrespect. The connections need to be understood more thoroughly than they are at present, and this seems to me to be an important project for scholarship and research into the nature of multicultural education.

NOTES AND REFERENCES

1. Appreciation to the Spencer Foundation for aid in supporting part of the research for this paper.
2. Cortner, Richard C. (1975) *The Supreme Court and Civil Liberties Policy* (Palo Alto: Mayfield), pp. 160–161.
3. Kymlicka, Will (1991) *Liberalism, Community and Culture* (Oxford: Clarendon Press). For another excellent treatment of the issue of cultural rights from a different view, see Yael Tamir (1993) *Liberal Nationalism* (Princeton: Princeton University Press).
4. Sandel, Michael J. (1982) *Liberalism and the Limits of Justice* (Cambridge: Cambridge University Press), pp. 58–59.
5. In contrast, say, to an expanded public realm where shared facilities reduce dependency on private wealth.
6. See Kymlicka, *op. cit.*, pp. 136–181.
7. See Feinberg, Walter (1993) *Japan and the Pursuit of a New American Identity: Work and Education in a Multicultural Age* (New York: Routledge). This and section VII are drawn from that book. See pp. 168–198 for an extended treatment of these themes.
8. Shweder, Richard A. (1991) *Thinking Through Cultures: Expeditions in Cultural Psychology* (Cambridge, MA: Harvard University Press), p. 191.
9. MacIntyre, Alasdair (1988) *Whose Justice? Which Rationality?* (Notre Dame, IN: Notre Dame University Press), ch. XIX.

Runes and Ruins: teaching reading cultures

AMÉLIE OKSENBERG RORTY

Think of the absurdity of representing the culture of the United States to schoolchildren in Ulan Bator by giving them some translations of Walt Whitman, Louisa May Alcott and Martin Luther King, showing them a John Wayne Western followed by a Fourth of July celebration, complete with flags, speeches, hot dogs and firecrackers. It is equally absurd to represent the complex dynamics of contemporary Mexican culture by some slides of Diego Rivera frescoes, a few translations of Carlos Fuentes' essays and a staged costume party, complete with a mariachi band, tacos and piñatas. With the best of intentions, many multicultural programmes introduce appreciative 'readings' in a Classic Comic format in hopes of promoting the cultural identity and the self-esteem of Mexican-African-Native-American schoolchildren. The complex interactions between cultures and the effects of multinational economics and international politics on ethnically defined 'cultures' are rarely analysed. When some attempt is made to place those works in their historical and political contexts, the story tends to be told as an ideologically charged morality tale: it is either a tale of colonial exploitation or of the extension of democratic civility.

That is on the one hand. On the other hand, any slice of culture — not only *Walden* and *Beloved*, but also Main Street and Shopping Malls, the speeches of Farrakhan and the Sunday *New York Times Magazine* — can, when interpreted by a discerning mind, serve as a Rosetta Stone, an archaeological treasure capable of providing entry clues to a culture, to its elements, structure and the drama of its history. All works of culture — epics and satires, high and low art, election day speeches, architecture, festivals and holidays — present abundant material for interpretation. But understanding the details of these monuments — seeing why there is an arch here, an allusion to Job there — does not differentiate the boundaries or describe the terrain of a single culture. 'The' culture of the United States is, like that of France and Italy, composed of motifs originally developed in Jerusalem, Athens, Constantinople and Cathay. Virtually all we think and all we do is composed of a palimpsest history of conquest, trade and exile that has formed our practices and evaluations. The details of any cultural work — a haunting song from a Magnum Opus, a desert mound of ruins, a cityscape — can be traced backwards and forward to distant places: their interpretation will yield riches that almost overwhelm the interpreter.

This by no means assures the possibility of constructing perspicuous translations across continental divides. Nor does it mean that cross-cultural importation can be prised loose from their contexts, as if there were a timeless cultural Esperanto that allows context-free borrowing. On the one hand, cultures are both diffuse and pervasively interactive. On the other, any viable culture is dynamically internally divided, encompassing radically distinct outlooks and insights. No matter how strict their Koranic interpretations may be, the literal understanding and observance of the Law in Isfahan does not coincide with those in Afghanistan or Malaysia. Even purist Islamic fundamentalists are affected and internally divided by local geopolitics. The internal geography of the culture of the United States is—as is that of any nation—as differentiated as are its sources: despite TV and the Knicks, the culture of urban Detroit can hardly be assimilated to that of Thomasville, Georgia or Peerless, Montana.[1] As it lives and breathes, the culture of a nation's military corps is distinguishable from that of its mercantile class, and both from that of the High Priests (whoever they may be). There may be some highly general—not to say vague—consensus about the basic style and directions of a culture, but these are likely to be ambiguous, usefully open to distinctive interpretations by those with opposed interests. In any case, determining the primary directions of a culture's morality or its style sets the scene of a political battlefield: claims to cultural descriptions are claims to the ruling high territory.

The varieties of issues that arise in debates over multicultural education—particularly when they are focused on defining the canon—displace the proper directions of our attention: we are deflected away from the issues that should concern us. In their present form, these debates make four crucial mistakes, mistakes that lead educators away from their proper tasks and activities. *First* they presuppose a highly suspect cultural essentialism; *secondly* they misrepresent the aims of a cosmopolitan education; *thirdly* they distort criteria for constructing a sound curriculum; and *fourthly* they offer a woefully inadequate pedagogic model of the processes of interpretive reading.

First, the essentialism implicit in these debates masks the conflicts among the heterogeneous associations that constitute vibrant populations; it disguises the dynamic interactions among the allied and conflicting groups of a complex society. Economic classes, ethnic groups, age cohorts, genders, religious organisations, races, occupations each claim to define the primary interests and directions of the shifting 'identifications' and 'identities' of their members.[2] Each group claims to represent the dominant aims and interests of its members, independently of their other alliances; each claims to represent the objective interests of the others; each is itself internally divided; each claims to represent the entirety of the culture to the world at large.[3] The continuous power struggles among these groups have powerful implications for educational policy: each claims to have the right to form educational policy, to have the right of curricular representation if not also of curricular determination.

What is included in the study of a culture? (Does it include a nation's military history? Does it encompass the motives and aspirations that are generated by a multinational market economy? Does it include the works of alienated expatriates, for instance the novels of Salman Rushdie or the poetry of non-observant anti-Zionist Israeli Jews who have emigrated to Australia?) How are cultures differentiated? (Is there a German-American culture, a German-Jewish-American culture and a Ladies'-Garment-Worker-German-Jewish-American culture? Is the pre-Castro-Cuban-American culture identical with that of the post-Castro-Cuban-American culture? Is the culture of an Appalachian subsistence farmer identical with that of a Wall Street broker? The culture of a widowed Iranian peasant woman with that of Ayatollah Khomeni?) Who is entitled to represent 'the identity' of a culture? The implicit essentialism in most multicultural programmes disguises the politics that stand behind specific characterisations: they typically do not reveal the reconstructive and politically charged, often divisive, battles over such representations. (Who should design the Latin American section of the curriculum in Texas schools? The Mexican cultural attaché? The multinational Tex-Mex corporate executives who sit on regional School Boards? The first-grade school teacher in Los Arrobles, Texas?)

Secondly, what is the implicit aim of multicultural representation, as it directs criteria for inclusion and exclusion of curricular materials? Charles Taylor has argued for the propriety, and indeed the obligation, of introducing multicultural education in a liberal democracy.[4] Taylor argues that individuals are, at least in part, constituted by their cultural identities. Because the state is charged with providing the basic conditions for citizen self-determination, it is also charged with protecting and promoting the legitmate self-defining activities of the groups through which its citizens structure their identities. The identity politics of celebratory mutual recognition is designed to enhance the indentificatory self-esteem of the members of subcultures. The politics of mutual recognition — the role of 'the look of the other' in forming the kind of self-respecting self-consciousness that Taylor thinks is a precondition for active civic participation — is the liberal grandchild of Hegel's analysis of the master-slave relation.

But however liberating self-consciousness and self-respect may be, they are neither necessary nor sufficient for genuine, enlightened civic participation. While they sometimes provide an important enabling contribution, self-regarding attitudes are only as good as the competence — the knowledge and skills essential to empowerment — on which they depend. Cultural studies sometimes enhance respect and self-respect, and sometimes they do not; self-respect sometimes enhances morally sensitive political activity, and sometimes it does not. The history of Western Europe is, as we are often rightly reminded, unlikely to promote the respect or self-respect of Americans of European descent: it would be surprising if African, Asian and Latin American history were radically different. Honest and complex interpretations of cultures sometimes give specific grounds for celebration, but they also provide abundant material for shame, grief and anguish.

Thirdly, educational institutions and practices provide the primary terrain for securing the politics of multicultural recognition. The importance of a cosmopolitan sophistication in promoting an active civic participation certainly argues for a rigorous expansion of the curriculum. The question is: just how should a curriculum be expanded?

Those who — for a variety of reasons — argue for an expansion of multicultural education are surely right that we are, on the whole, woefully ignorant about the societies and cultures that have contributed to the amalgam of populations in the United States.[5] But they are typically mistaken about reasons for revising our curriculum, and wrong, too, about the directions that this correction should take. The debates about whether to expand or to preserve the canon disguise the rationale that should direct the proper expansion of our pitifully narrow, introverted curriculum. Considering how profoundly and dangerously ignorant we are of Asian and African history, of the literature and the geopolitics of Latin America — how unable we are to communicate in Spanish, Chinese or German — no one could reasonably object to a policy mandating language requirements and cultural studies in the curricula of public schools. But the best argument for extending our linguistic repertoire and expanding the curriculum is not that those studies will conduce to cultural or individual self-respect. A liberal state should promote serious cross-cultural studies in the public schools because ignorance is manifestly politically dangerous and being monolingual is only one step away from being mute.

We cannot hope to understand ourselves — and still less make wise political decisions — without understanding the values, the politics and economics that mark our global neighbours. While the kind of appreciative sampling of multicultural folklore, sacred texts and major literary works now favoured in most kindergartens and many universities hardly qualifies as genuine cultural study, it can provide a beginning that should be used to serve as an introduction to serious geopolitical and cultural analysis. Since folklore and sacred texts typically encode references to highly divisive sociopolitical controversies, interpreting them aright leads directly to anthropology and to political history.

This does not mean that we should 'reduce' works to politics or social psychology or even to the anxiety of poetic influence. 'When lilacs last in the doorway bloomed' is not usefully understood as a homosexual response to the Civil War, nor is the ritual surrounding a piñata best understood as a brilliant device for promoting the economic benefits of local crafts. In designing the curriculum, we should attempt to avoid reductionism of any and every sort, including the insouciant reductionist flattening of the kind of post-modernist readings that decontextualise the bits and pieces that have formed us, and whose substantive interpretation informs and enriches us.

Although the issues that drive the numerous controversies about the canon are extremely various, they all represent the modern version of Swift's battle of the books. Both the critics and the defenders of the existing core canon of educational classics are guilty of an odd form of idolatry: they treat books as if they were powerful ikons, to be either revered or defaced.[6] Defenders argue that those works represent our best and most estimable achievements: the hope of civility rests in our preserving and appropriating them. Critics want either to widen the representation of saints, or to show that the ikons of the Western classics are worm-eaten.

Fourthly, the battle of the books extends to the *ways* we recognise 'otherness'. Interpretive reading — of events, architecture and persons as well as books — does not consist of ever more finely discriminating appreciation; it does not involve treating books and events as engraved texts, inter-texts or subtexts.[7] When we are lost in the admiration — or the exposure — of a perfectly polished text, reading does not enlarge and empower us. Adding Luxun, Borges and Achebe to the pantheon of heroic literary achievement does not by itself promote either the sense or the skills of civic participation that public education should develop. Chinese-American and Chicano-American children will not become self-respecting active citizens by becoming passive consumers of their cultural achievements. Like all readers, they should rather become actively engaged in the work — the uncertainties and struggles — of interpreting as a form of action. Even scientific works like Galileo's *Two New Sciences* or philosophical works like Descartes' *Meditations* — let alone *The Federalist Papers*, Luxun's stories or Borges' fantastic construction — are best understood as attempts to integrate novel (as yet barely understood) intuitions with inherited (barely recognised) assumptions. Learning to read well is an absolutely essential preparation for participation in the melée of political and cultural activity, not primarily because it informs or inspires, but because the searching activities of interpretive reading are, at their best, also exercised in political life. Reading does not separate a stage of appreciative empathic immersion followed by a stage of externalised objective judgement; it merges tact, resourceful improvisation and criticism in the detective work of deciphering unstated questions and preoccupations. It locates uncertainties and unresolved tensions, tracing strategies of inventive reconciliation among the varied directions of authorial (agent) purposes; it understands where — and why — negotiated resolutions fail; it projects the inheritance of problems that authors pose for their successors.

All we do in the way of writing and making is, and must be understood as, work-in-progress, work struggling to integrate — to weave together — the multiple and diverse strands that compose us: economic practices and religious images, geopolitical history, science and science fiction. Although it also essentially involves perspectival perception, a cultural work is not best understood on the model of representation or presentation. It is a struggle to integrate, reconcile, propitiate and attack the past; it is a response to contemporary colleagues and enemies; it is an attempt to form the future. What we have deplorably come to call 'texts', and treated as runes and ruins are, in truth, activities. They are private and collective, artistic and political 'workings through'. Reading these works requires participating in them, re-enacting the process by which they emerged, locating the problems that impelled their expression and construction.

Appropriately read, the traditional canon is multicultural: Herodotus brings us immediately to Egypt and the far reaches of the Nile; Marco Polo takes us to Cathay; to understand Flaubert and Henry James, we must trace their travels; and as Edward Sa'id — a powerful critic of narrow readings of the canon — has recently amply demonstrated, a close and careful reading of Jane Austen lands us right in the colonial empire. Inappropriately read, the works of Allende and Mahfouz become scented sachets, objects of the kind of sighing sentimentality that these authors abhor; inappropriately read, Achebe is reduced to an anti-colonial propagandist, and Naipaul is charged with cultural betrayal. This does not, of course, mean that we can get all the benefits of multiculturalism by staying right at home, continuing to force-feed students with Bowdlerised (de-Nietzsched) versions of Emerson and Thoreau; nor does it mean that we should treat cultural works as textbooks for International Civics 202. It means that we should understand that teaching reading cultures involves luring our students to become active interpreters rather than passive consumers of Kulchur. It means engaging them in the role-playing tasks of (re)constructive detection, placing themselves in the position of working author/agents.[8]

NOTES AND REFERENCES

1. Yes, Virginia, there is a Thomasville, Georgia and a Peerless, Montana.
2. See Amelie Rorty, Varieties of pluralism in a polyphonic society, *Review of Metaphysics*, 1990; Amelie Rorty and David Wong, Aspects of identity and agency, in: Owen Flanagan (ed.) *Identity, Character and Morality* (Cambridge MA: MIT, 1990).
3. See my The hidden politics of cultural identification, *Political Theory*, 1994 and Amy Gutmann, The challenge of Multiculturalism in political ethics, *Philosophy and Public Affairs*, 1993; and the essays of Gutmann and Susan Wolf in Charles Taylor *et al.*, *Multiculturalism and 'The Politics of Recognition'* (Princeton, 1992).
4. Charles Taylor, *The Ethics of Authenticity* (Cambridge, MA: Harvard University Press, 1992). For a trenchant assessment of Taylor's recent work, see Arthur Danto's review in *The Times Literary Supplement*, January 29th 1993.
5. Asian and African students at the Harvard Graduate School of Education have a standing joke about the curriculum in the School. For every serious course on anthropology and international affairs, they say, there are four courses (count 'em!) on the importance of multicultural education. For their part, Latin American students joke about the self-deceptive naivety revealed by all parties to these discussions—multiculturalists and traditionalists alike—referring to the curriculum of *American* schools, thereby unselfconsciously appropriating Canada and the whole of Latin America.
6. Swift's 'The Battle of the Books between the Ancients and the Moderns' provides a nice analogue of current controversies about the multicultural expansion of the canon. See also David Bromwich, *Politics By Other Means: Higher Education and Group Thinking* (New Haven: Yale, 1992) and thoughtful, provocative reviews of that book by Alan Ryan (*New York Review of Books*, February 1993) and Jeremy Waldron, (*Times Literary Supplement*, January 22nd 1993).
7. See John Searle, *New York Review of Books*, 6 December 1990.
8. This paper is a descendant of my The hidden politics of cultural identification, *Political Theory*, 1994. It is the parent of my Rights: educational, not cultural, *Social Research*, 1995.

Multiculturalism for the Religious Right?
Defending Liberal Civic Education

STEPHEN MACEDO

I. INTRODUCTION

A growing number of scholars and ordinary citizens believe that contemporary liberal political regimes — in their educational policies and their politics more broadly — promote a 'culture of disbelief' by unfairly silencing, marginalising or ignoring the religious voice in the public square, and my failing adequately to accommodate the free exercise of religion. Such charges are not *all* wrong. The long and meticulous reach of the modern welfare state, and insufficient popular respect for the practices of minority religions, may sometimes leave too little room for people to practise their religious beliefs. There are, moreover, 'evangelical' secularists who would, under the banner of liberal politics and democratic education, seek to undermine religious life.[1]

And yet today's champions of greater solicitude for religious believers and communities are too often uncritical in their embrace of religious diversity. Those who would open wider the public square to religion sometimes give short shrift to the basic political need to make sure that religion is tamed and made compatible with the imperative of peaceful coexistence amid diversity.

I will allow that we may sometimes have good reason to accommodate religious practices and communities to a greater extent than we do. We should, in addition, support multicultural education if it means affirming that there are many reasonable and respectable cultural and religious traditions that make important contributions to the well-being of their adherents and the shared good of modern liberal democracies. I want to urge, however, that we should not entertain false hopes of what we can or should seek to achieve in this endeavour. In particular, I want to defend the spirit of liberal institutions and practices that do indeed marginalise religion to some degree, at least from the perspective of our political life.

The scope of this paper is limited by its focus on the problem of accommodating and extending multicultural respect to *religious* diversity, and by its concentration on the *American* context. The issues I canvass are, however, relevant to the wider problem of multiculturalism. If the United States stands as one relatively successful model for those who would seek to forge political unity out of religious, ethnic, cultural, racial and other forms of diversity, that success is neither secure nor complete. Religious communities remain, in America as elsewhere, a potent source of complaint about liberal educational policies and practices. The temptation uncritically to extend multicultural concern to religious communities is not confined to America.

II. RELIGIOUS FUNDAMENTALISTS VERSUS CIVIC EDUCATION?

In America, the most dramatic clashes between the state's interest in civic education and claims for religious diversity typically occur in public schools. I want to begin by considering an example of the temptation to go to excessive lengths to accommodate religious complaints in the name of extending multicultural concern to the political right. The case in question, Mozert *v.* Hawkins (which I have dealt with at some length elsewhere[2]), is interesting not simply for the legal and moral issues it raises, but as an important recent episode in what has become known in the United States as our 'culture war'. This 'war' typically pits liberal intellectuals, proponents of democratic education and other cosmopolitan types against local communities of religious believers and, increasingly, their intellectual defenders from across the political spectrum.[3] Not everyone has chosen sides in this war, happily, and one of the things I want to do here is to defend a tough-minded but moderate version of liberalism (drawing on the recent account provided by John Rawls) that offers some middle ground.[4]

In *Mozert*, some fundamentalist and evangelical religious families in a rural Tennessee school district took issue on a whole variety of grounds with a series of textbooks used in reading classes in grades one to eight. The books were alleged to promote a variety of things the families found objectionable, including telepathy, witchcraft, evolution and 'women's liberation'. The most interesting charge, however, and the one that has drawn important and sympathetic scholarly attention, was that the readers interfered with the free exercise of the families' religion by exposing the children to a variety of religious points of view in an even-handed manner, thus denigrating the truth of their particular religious beliefs.[5]

The *Mozert* families at first sought to ban the offending books from the schools, but later asked to have their children excused from the reading programme while otherwise remaining in the public schools (the families offered to comply with state reading requirements on their own, with the children taking the same standardised tests as other public school children). The school district eventually refused to allow the children to opt out, and made the reading programme mandatory, suspending those children who would not comply. The parents challenged the school board in court, claiming that the policy denied their right to the 'free exercise' of their religious beliefs (which is protected by the first Amendment of the US Constitution[6]). The families lost their case on appeal in federal court.

Mozert has furnished an occasion for some at both the liberal and conservative ends of the political spectrum to argue that greater accommodation of fundamentalists should be undertaken in the name of a fair-minded extension of multicultural concern to the political right. Well, why not? At first blush, accommodation of religious objections looks like the most 'liberal' position. Liberalism is about pluralism, religious freedom and individual choice, after all, so how could a liberal refuse to accommodate a dissident religious minority like the *Mozert* litigants?

There are problems, however, with the leap to accommodate. Consider the position taken by Stephen Bates, an intelligent and sophisticated observer who has written a splendid account of *Mozert* which, however, not only displays an over-eagerness to accommodate but does so on grounds that must furnish deep misgivings. Bates approvingly quotes a remark of two British educators:

> What makes a particular culture identifiably that culture might include essentially sexist or racist practices and principles . . . Sexism can be, in theory, rooted in beliefs which are among the most strongly held and which are crucial to cultural identity. That is, they can be the very sort of belief which those of us who value a multicultural society think that minorities have the right to preserve.[7]

Bates defends accommodation in *Mozert* because 'tolerating everything except intolerance is circular. As Tom Lehrer once put it, "I know there are people in the world who do not love their fellow men. And I hate people like that" '.[8]

We should pause before applauding Bates' proposed extension of multicultural concern to fundamentalists. This would be something to applaud only if the truest liberalism were one that refused to stand up even for liberal values. Such a stance misconceives the nature of our liberal political order, failing to see that liberalism is not grounded in an uncritical acceptance of diversity or the 'politics of difference'.[9] At base, liberalism is grounded in a shared commitment to a range of political values and practices: to tolerance and mutual respect for fellow citizens, at the very least, but also to a range of distinctively liberal virtues that include respect for the rule of law and the democratic process, a willingness to think critically about public affairs, and a willingness to affirm the supreme political authority of principles that we can justify in public from a point of view that we can share with reasonable fellow citizens of other religious faiths.[10]

Bates' view of liberal politics is far too undemanding. He insists that those who refuse to accommodate dissenting families and communities misunderstand the American Constitution and its liberal guarantees:

> The First Amendment requires the *state* to treat all faiths as equally valid. But citizens aren't obliged to follow suit. On the contrary: The separation of church and state is intended to safeguard each citizen's liberty to believe that his faith is valid and, if he chooses, that all others are heretical.[11]

The mistake here is in supposing that liberalism makes demands only on the state and not on citizens as well.

While it is true enough that our liberal Constitution protects the freedom to proclaim that the religious doctrines of others are heretical, that is not the end of it. Bates seems to forget that constitutionalism cannot endure without citizens who are willing to support its fundamental principles and to take part in defining them. We are citizens of a liberal democratic society, after all, not subjects of a state. Political power is our shared property and not something that is wielded over us. Liberal citizenship carries with it not only privileges but also obligations, including the obligation to respect the equal rights of fellow citizens whatever their faiths. One of the most basic forms of respect that we owe to fellow citizens is to offer them reasons for the way that we seek to shape the terrible coercive powers of the state, reasons that they can share even while disagreeing with us about religion.[12]

Of course, people remain free to practise their religion, and that freedom includes the right to condemn alternative belief systems. The lives of liberal citizens are properly divided: we have a public and a private side, and the public or political side is guided by imperatives designed to make our shared life together possible. On the public side we should put aside our religious convictions—at least when shaping the most basic rights and political principles—in the sense of acknowledging the political authority of reasons and principles we can hold in common as a political community. Political power is, in this way, thought of as a trust held in common (held by us all in our capacity as fellow citizens), which we may not dispose of for our private purposes.

Aside from the shared obligations of our political role as citizens, we also count on our political institutions and practices to help harmonise our differences over the course of time. Diversity is often a value, and we will often have good reasons to make exceptions for those whose religious views or other basic convictions are out of the mainstream. Differences of religious conviction do not, however, harmonise automatically: peaceful coexistence is an achievement, not a foregone conclusion. Promoting mutual respect for rights is importantly the work of schools, political institutions and our constitutional order as a whole (people are educated not only directly but indirectly in a host of ways), and that important work sometimes requires that we do *not* give in to calls for accommodation or exemption.

Those who rush, whether from left or right, to embrace multiculturalism forget that liberal citizens do not come into existence naturally. Diversity must be constituted for liberal democratic purposes. We have no reason to apologise for taking reasonable measures to promote the political supremacy of liberal democratic values, or for educating children towards the virtues needed by liberal citizens.

With respect to the objections advanced in *Mozert*, we must remember that children cannot be good citizens of a diverse liberal polity unless they are taught that critical thinking and public argument—reason-giving and reason-demanding in public—are the appropriate means of political justification. Children must, moreover, be exposed to the religious diversity that constitutes our polity for the sake of learning to respect as fellow citizens those who differ with them in matters of religion. The crucial thing is that their civic education should be guided by *civic* imperatives: the question of religious truth should simply be left aside. Children must be taught that all religions are equal in the eyes of the state; whether they are equal in the eyes of God is a matter about which liberal public authorities should have nothing to say. Public institutions may teach the importance of critical thinking as a path to political reasonableness and good citizenship, but must leave aside the question of how one arrives at religious truth. By following these strictures, public institutions may help to inculcate liberal civic virtues while respecting the integrity of different religious claims. People are to be regarded as reasonable fellow citizens not because they espouse this or that religious view, but because they affirm shared political principles.

One might have hoped that the *Mozert* parents and the local school district could have worked out an accommodation without raising their conflict to the level of fundamental principle. Once raised to that level in a court of law, however, the right course was to deny the *Mozert* families their claimed right to opt out out of the reading programme. Surely exposing children to religious diversity in a reading programme, a history class or elsewhere is a prerequisite of any attempt to convey an accurate account of America's history and an appreciation of the political importance of toleration. If the state lacks the requisite authority to teach children about matters as central as these are to liberal politics, then we might as well concede that the liberal state has no educational authority in the face of religious objections. The complaint of the *Mozert* families was simply too sweeping, and too radically at odds with core aims of liberal civic education.[13]

No civic education can be neutral. A liberal civic education will, undoubtedly, make it harder for some parents to transmit their particular religious beliefs to their children. This will be the case most particularly for parents and religious communities with totalistic belief systems: those who would be guided by religious imperatives in all spheres of their lives, those who refuse to honour the political supremacy of reasons that can be shared with those outside one's church, as often seems the case with religious fundamentalists, such as the *Mozert* families. Communities oriented around totalistic belief systems may well be undermined when children become aware of the other religions that thrive side by side with their own, of the history of religious toleration and of the importance of respect for the rights of others and of critical thinking in politics. Totalistic belief systems may be undercut when children learn that while modern Western states are composed of many faiths and creeds, we share (at our best) one constitution. There is no necessary remedy for particular religious communities who lose members as a consequence of educational measures designed to help their children learn core liberal political values. We should be most reluctant, indeed, to grant a remedy when the group in question has not withdrawn from the world like the Amish and some other sects but is, like religious fundamentalism in America today, large, powerful and politically engaged. A price must be paid for life in a diverse society.

Here, I think, is where sensible defenders of liberal democracy must bite the bullet in a way that multiculturalists often refuse to do. A liberal order does not and should not guarantee a level playing field for all the religions and ways of life that people might adopt and sincerely espouse. That some people have a hard time passing on their convictions to their children in circumstances of peaceful, liberal diversity is not anything to apologise or (necessarily) to adjust for. We have no reason to be equally fair to those prepared to accept, and those who refuse to accept, the political authority of public reasons that fellow citizens can share.

The point of insisting that good liberal citizens should be prepared to put aside their religious convictions when publicly justifying basic principles of justice is not, it should be emphasised, to exclude religious citizens from the public realm.[14] We stick to shared grounds in politics because these are the only grounds that we can share while respecting the fact of deep and reasonable diversity in other matters. We do not, moreover, ask only religious people to put aside their ultimate ideals: ultimate secular ideals of life as a whole are just as reasonably disputable as religious ideals, and so these too must be put aside.

It is possible, of course, that the *Mozert* families might have offered a more moderate objection which might well have deserved a more respectful hearing. One could imagine public school readers, for example, *claiming* to teach respect for diversity while actually being filled with glowing portrayals of secular lives and grimly negative depictions of the follies of religious belief. While it would be unreasonable for anyone to insist on perfect balance and evenhandedness in any part of the curriculum, religious citizens who accept the political supremacy of liberal values may properly object to a state-sponsored educational regime that seems designed to disparage their deep, extra-political convictions at every turn.

Religious children are not the only ones who sometimes need lessons in toleration. There are zealots on behalf of secular philosophical ideals, people intent on using political means to impose their vision of the whole truth on the rest of the polity. Their children might also need to learn to respect fellow citizens with serious religious beliefs.

A liberal constitutional order is a complex rather than a simple system. We respect people's right to reject liberal democratic principles in both speech and practice — within limits. We can do this in part because our political regime is not neutral in its effects. We know that our political principles and practices are tilted against racists and religious zealots — including illiberal fundamental-ists — and so we can let them talk and organise, in the comforting knowledge that they are working against the grain of our system.

Simple versions of liberalism are to be avoided, especially in the vexing area of religious free exercise. We should want, if I am right, both to respect a broad range of private freedoms, and also to be resolute in the defence of liberal democratic public institutions and practices that are well-justified in public terms, even if they impose unequal burdens on some people. Versions of liberalisms committed to broad principles of neutrality or sweeping commitments to 'maximum feasible accommodation' of religious practice will be unable to do all the work that liberal consitutionalism needs to do.[15] Respect for freedom is central, but we also count on directly educative institutions and background practices that turn citizens towards the ways of the liberal regime, and these will non-neutrally constrain particular religious beliefs and practices. We should not lightly allow people to opt out of these arrangements.

We can now see that political liberalism entails a certain form of multicultural respect for a wide range of religious beliefs and deep philosophical convictions about the meaning of life. Political liberalism is not, after all, based on a single account of the whole truth of the human condition. It holds that all reasonable people will agree on certain fundamental principles of justice, which justify democratic political procedures and a range of basic freedoms, but it does not assert the truth of one account of the meaning of life as a whole. It insists at the very base, indeed, that there are *many* reasonable answers to the deepest questions of meaning and value, many reasonable religious and philosophical views of mankind's highest ends. When it comes to justifying basic rights and principles of justice, good liberal citizens leave aside their conceptions of the truth as a whole, and seek ground they can share with fellow citizens with different creeds.

Political liberalism is a form of multiculturalism. It is, crucially, a *critical* and *politically acute* form of multiculturalism which does not sell short the project of forging a shared political framework. Political liberalism is a pluralistic form of multiculturalism: a stance that acknowledges the contributions of many diverse cultural traditions and religious communities to our shared life together while honouring (and taking measures to ensure the supremacy of) the supreme political authority of a shared point of view and the values it justifies — systematic values that overarch our differences and allow us to live together peacefully.[16] Political liberalism furnishes principled grounds for not supporting those who insist on the whole truth of their particular cultural or religious belief system at the expense of a system of mutually respectful liberal multiculturalism.

III. LIBERAL DEMOCRACY AS CULTURE OF DISBELIEF?

Bates is not the only commentator who is too uncritical in extending special solicitude to religious believers in the name of multiculturalism. Stephen Carter defends a broader form of this solicitude in his widely discussed book, *Culture of Disbelief*. Carter's argument, not unlike that of Bates, is a confluence of two powerful intellectual streams: the traditional respect for religious pluralism and (as above) the newer rhetoric of multiculturalism.

My disagreement with Carter is not really with his position on any particular policy matter. He does not advocate particularly unusual or outrageous policy measures. His book evinces, however, a general lack of political tough-mindedness with respect to the question of religious diversity. In his laudable concern to take the perspective of the believer more seriously than academics often do, Carter shortchanges the perspective of the citizen of our shared political order. As a consequence, he also embraces a form of multiculturalism that is deeply illiberal.

There are often, of course, good grounds for making special accommodations for the freedom of religious communities and believers, and Carter enumerates a number of these:

— Religious communities are important intermediate associations — 'separate heads of sovereignty'[17] — that keep the danger of majority tyranny in check. Members of religious communities will be prepared to resist the authority of the state and of public opinion — sometimes for ill (as when religious zealots murder doctors who perform abortions) but more often for good (as with the Abolitionists and the Civil Rights movement).
— Religions often challenge, in particular, the materialism, hedonism and this-worldliness which is so dominant in our time.
— Religions furnish alternative sources of meaning which keep alive the

intellectual arguments by which truth is supposedly approached in a liberal polity. John Stuart Mill famously argued in *On Liberty* that society needed 'bold atheists', independent thinkers to prevent dominant belief systems from becoming dead dogmas. It may be that nowadays — at least in intellectual circles — the dead intellectual dogma is liable to be secularism or scepticism. Carter argues that today's independent thinkers challenging received orthodoxies are the religious believers.[18]

— To unfairly marginalize and silence religious believers — who after all include the vast majority of ordinary Americans — is to fan their alienation and resentment, to encourage their disaffection with our political system and even to provoke revolution.[19]

— Finally, and very importantly, Carter insists that we remember the political context within which we are operating in late twentieth-century Western nations, with their vast and pervasively intrusive welfare and regulatory bureaucracies. Accommodation and exception-making for religious believers may not have been very important in the nineteenth century when states — especially centralized national states — were so minimal and constrained. Things today are different. Accommodating religious practice is especially important now lest the ever-encroaching tentacles of state control choke off the space which autonomous communities require.

These are important and powerful reasons for taking seriously the project of accommodation. They are reasons that cohere nicely with the aims of liberalism, for they highlight the contribution that religious communities make to our shared life together. They are not, however, reasons to adopt an uncritical accommodationist stance towards religious communities that seek exemptions from generally applicable policies. Unfortunately, Carter goes beyond these sensible grounds.

Carter complains repeatedly, for example, that liberalism requires serious religious believers to 'split their public and private selves', telling them that 'it is fine to be religious in private, but there is something askew when those private beliefs become the basis of public action'.[20] Liberals will regard as weird or dangerous those who submit to religious authority in every aspect of their lives: in deciding where to buy a house, whether to get married and even whom to marry. Many liberals will only be happy, Carter argues, if believers treat their religion as a hobby: discrete, unimportant and confined to the weekend.[21]

The reason for all this in the American context, Carter repeatedly suggests, is to be found in the partisan imperatives of politics post-Roe *v.* Wade (the case that struck down the abortion laws of all 50 states and established the broad but not unlimited right of women to decide whether to have an abortion).[22] Since Roe *v.* Wade, religious involvement in our politics is identified with the religious right, so 'liberals' (now meaning those on the political left) argue for the exclusion of religion from politics while conservatives tend to welcome this involvement. But this is shortsighted, Carter insists, for religious communities have played an important role in many liberal crusades, including the abolition of slavery and the Civil Rights movement. Religious involvement in politics is, Carter claims, usually a force for good.[23]

When Carter suggests that the 'liberal' opposition to political action directed at religious aims is based on the imperatives of partisan politics after *Roe*, he conflates two different meanings of 'liberal': the narrower partisan designation of the political left (especially in America), and the older and broader meaning that unites most Americans and Europeans. The broad liberal social contract tradition, going back at least to John Locke, argues that for political authority to be legitimate it should be capable of being justified on the basis of reasons and principles that fellow citizens can hold in common. It was not Ted Kennedy or some other icon of the political left who insisted that the church is

a thing absolutely separate and distinct from the Commonwealth. The boundaries on both sides are fixed and immovable. He jumbles heaven and earth together, the things most remote and opposite, who mixes these two societies; which are in their original, end, business, and every thing, perfectly distinct and infinitely different from each other.

John Locke, the greatest liberal of them all, argued this three centuries ago in his *Letter Concerning Toleration*.[24]

In politics, we should focus on things of the body rather than of the soul, not because the former is more important but because our most basic interests in this world converge to a greater extent than our beliefs about the next. Of course, we are not all equally interested in peace or health or freedom or prosperity. Putting aside spiritual matters will not make everyone equally happy, but for this there is no remedy.

Interestingly, the examples Carter chooses to illustrate the benefits of religious involvement in politics suggest that he may not be entirely convinced of his own argument, for those examples pay implicit homage to the political authority of shared reasons. There were good public reasons, after all, for abolishing slavery and extending civil rights to black Americans. Sensible liberals will have no reason to oppose those who organise their religious communities against publicly defined and justified injustices. The central liberal concern is not with rooting out religious *motives*, but rather with ensuring that there are adequate *public reasons* that justify the way we seek to use political power. There will often be *additional* religious reasons and motives for well-justified political activity, and that is not a problem. The important thing is that we all acknowledge that the proper test of just political aims is not a religious test but the test of public reason. Carter's examples (if not his argument) suggest that after all he may agree.[25]

Happily, many on both the right and the left of our politics agree that our most basic rights and liberties should be resolved on the basis of reasons and evidence that can be shared by the political community. When Rev. Jerry Falwell and most other leaders of the American religious right argue that abortion is murder, they typically do so not in terms of particular scriptural interpretations that appeal only to co-religionists, but in terms of grounds that can be shared with fellow citizens who reject their particular religious views. That is all to the good.

Of course, Carter is right to suppose that *some* religious people will have a hard time separating their religious and their public selves. Some people have a hard time recognising the political authority of reasons that can be shared with fellow citizens of different faiths. Carter's mistake is in supposing that this means something is wrong with liberalism. People who refuse to move outside their sectarian perspective cannot be good citizens of a pluralistic liberal society (in this respect at least).

Having said this, let us also note that those who insist on attempting to shape basic rights and liberties in accordance with sectarian imperatives will not (as Carter and others suggest) be 'silenced' in any literal sense by liberals. When liberal theorists or courts argue that citizens should have public justifications for the way they seek to use political power, they are not suggesting that those who violate these strictures should be denied First Amendment rights to speak and publish. No liberal suggests that those who disagree should be silenced: religious zealots are free to use their liberal rights improperly to argue that the constitution should reflect the will of God.

The 'silencing' that Carter complains of is no more than what passes for the genuine article in today's language of victimology: people are 'silenced' when other people disagree with them. More specifically, and even less plausibly, Carter seems to worry that religious people are silenced when others insist that it is wrong to invoke religious reasons and arguments as justifications for coercing people in a pluralistic society. While Carter argues that religious communities are centres of 'resistance' to the state, this resistance is apparently rather anaemic.

The language of 'silencing' is a poor metaphor for what liberals propose, but it reveals something important about those who level such charges. It is evidently not enough for Carter and others that the rights of religious people to speak and profess are respected. He complains that the public square is 'formally open' but 'religious witness is not welcomed there'.[26] In the same vein, Carter argues that *tolerance* of religion is not enough:

> Tolerance without respect means little; if I tolerate you but do not respect you, the message of my tolerance, day after day, is that *my* forbearance, not *your* right, and certainly not *the nation's* commitment to equality, frees you to practice your religion. You do it by my sufferance, but not with my approval.[27]

This appears strangely confused. What citizens are called upon to respect are rights, not the way that people use their rights, as in: 'I respect your right to talk bloody nonsense and will defend it to the death, but I certainly do not approve of the drivel you propose'. It would be self-defeating to demand more than this, for the whole point of our freedom is to allow us to disagree vehemently but peacefully.

The strained metaphor of 'silencing' and the strange confusion of rights and respect both suggest that what Carter wants to protect is not the freedom to disagree vigorously, but a psychological fragility and sensitivity on the part of religious believers that is inconsistent with vigorous disagreement. How strange this is for someone such as Carter, who celebrates the 'subversive independence' of religious communities and their ability to 'mobilize passions' as opposed to reason, and who denies that we should try to 'domesticate' them.[28] All this tough rhetoric turns out to be mainly bluster: Carter's believers are an oddly timid lot. They seek not only liberty but approval, not simply the right to speak but a welcome mat at the public square. They cower at the prospect of being burned at the stake of public disapproval.

Elsewhere, this solicitude for sensitive psyches leads Carter to conflate intellectual disagreement and physical vulnerability. He goes so far as to portray proselytising as a method of wiping people 'off the face of the earth'. 'I have even heard it suggested', says Carter,

> that the idea that Christians should tolerate Jews developed hand-in-glove with the notion that Christians should try to persuade them to come to Christ. It is hard to be happy if one's religious choice is tolerated only in order to hasten its destruction. America should put no one to that choice. A vital security of life in a free society should be that, far from being tolerated, every religious person and every religious group can claim equal rights with every other.[29]

It makes all the difference in the world, of course, whether someone seeks to 'destroy' a religion through voluntary conversion or force. Carter resists this basic distinction, however, and once again seems to want 'equal concern and respect', not simply for persons' rights as citizens, but for what every person believes and regards as valuable.

The combination of radicalism and sensitivity here is troubling, but far from unheard of in defences of multiculturalism. On the one hand, Carter insists that religions are subversively and passionately independent. They are moved by 'religious ways of knowing that are relegated to inferior status' by contemporary American liberalism.[30] And yet these supposedly brave souls are so fragile as to be 'silenced' by disapproval and intimidated by attempts at persuasion and conversion. Cherishing our 'epistemic diversity', for Carter, seems to mean not only ignoring the political authority of shared reasons, but also requiring everyone to be non-judgmental with respect to other people's ideas.[31]

To combine respect for diversity with a great concern for mutual sensitivity to offence, as Carter does, is a prescription for illiberality. Carter cares so much for protecting sensitive egos from the upsets of criticism and disapproval that he brands serious disagreement and efforts at persuasion or conversion as forms of intolerance. Ironically, then, it is Carter who would 'silence' vigorous disagreement in the name of his multiculturalism of mutual sensitivity.

Liberalism separates the spheres of religion and politics, and asks people to divide their lives in order to make possible a peaceful framework within which individuals and groups can fight vigorously for their beliefs. In politics we acknowledge the authority of a shared point of view, but when it comes to religious and cultural matters we are free to disagree deeply. Yet Carter pleads for deference towards those who refuse to distance themselves from their religious convictions, those who refuse to 'split' their religious and political selves.

The call for deference and sensitivity towards those with totalistic belief systems may contribute to the ascription of psychological fragility to religious citizens. It is precisely those citizens who cannot separate their political status as equal citizens from their particular religious convictions who will have the hardest time seeing that people can vigorously disagree about religion while respecting one another as fellow citizens. Such 'undivided' selves will have a hard time recognising that 'attacks' on their religion or culture in no way undermine their status as citizen with rights.

Totalistic belief systems seem, therefore, a prescription for feelings of vulnerability in conditions of diversity. Since deep religious and cultural pluralism seem to be with us for good, the last thing we should do is join Carter and some other multiculturalists in encouraging these sensitivities by giving them legal force.

There is a final irony of Carter's overall stance, which only reinforces and makes more troubling the illiberal tendencies implicit in his position. While his book is laced with references to the bible and his own religious beliefs — all of which are admittedly rare in an academic work — he also rather oddly seems to embrace a radical postmodern relativism. He praises 'epistemic diversity' and insists that 'given its starting point and methodology, creationism is as rational an explanation as any other' (there is an awful lot built into that 'given', but we will leave that aside).[32] The battle between creationism and those who defend evolutionary accounts of human origins is a 'war between competing systems of discerning truth'. The victor in this battle, Carter seems to suggest, can be determined not by better reasons or superior insight but only by 'power'.[33]

This postmodernist attitude towards truth may help to explain both why Carter seems drawn towards the multiculturalism of mutual sensitivity, and why such a position is so deeply at odds with liberalism. Liberals typically support the rule of public reason, after all, because they believe that public argument, debate and reason-giving really do help us to distinguish better and worse answers. As indicated above, moreover, we have special reasons in diverse democratic polities for regarding as authoritative reasons that we can present, criticise and share in public as a community.

For Carter, however, deep disagreements are clashes of rival epistemologies or world-views without any way of judging among them. Carter seems to have come round to the position of Stanley Fish and others that the faith in public reason represents nothing more than a powerful but contestable way of seeing the world with no special or privileged claim to knowledge, no more than one ultimate faith among others.[34] Given all this, we might as well surrender to those who resist a political programme dedicated to critical thinking and public reason: we have no reason to regard these latter practices as having any special authority. All of this helps to explain why Carter favours public sensitivity and equality of respect over robust argument. Robust argument would seem to have no point in the postmodernist universe. Where would it get us? It cannot allow us to discern better and more justifiable positions; it is only 'our' way of asserting our power.

It is hardly surprising, then, that Carter explicitly links multiculturalism to calls for the inclusion of creationism in the curriculum. If there are only disparate and conflicting world-views with no means of adjudicating among them, why not treat them all as equally valid? Carter is simply being fair-minded in recognising that creationists have as much claim to be accommodated as the favoured constituencies of the political left.[35]

There is a further step in this march toward Babel that is sometimes taken by the wackier multiculturalists (or perhaps I should simply say the consistently radical ones) and it is hard to see how Carter could resist it. If creationism has an equal claim to legitimacy with mainstream science, then so presumably do voodoo, witchcraft and other superstitions. If the world is divided into merely *different* 'world-views', and not better and worse ones, then any notion, however kooky, if maintained consistently (well, why make a fetish of consistency?) or as part of a 'way of life', merits multicultural respect.

The radical multicultural march away from public reason is a march away from liberalism. If liberal claims to public authority rest on nothing more than superior power, then one cannot be said to have good reasons to favour liberal arrangements over the rivals: favouring individual rights and robust public argument is only a matter of taste and ultimately of power. Of course, if all we have in the end is a war of all against all, with no privileged claims to authority and no shared public standards for adjudicating among conflicting claims, then Hobbes may have been right to suppose that straightforward tyranny is the safest course. But then, if the postmodernists are right that liberalism is after all a soft and disguised form of tyranny, I suppose that sensible Hobbesians will be content to live with it.

Neither Carter nor other multiculturalists favour anything so hard as Hobbesian authoritarianism (and much of what I have ascribed to Carter is merely implicit in his position). We can however see the germs of a soft form of intolerance in Carter's intellectual stance, an intellectual intolerance characteristic of some forms of multiculturalism. These germs are precisely the overriding desire to protect fragile egos from the upsets of criticism and judgement, the insistence on mutual respect and a postmodernist scepticism about the possibility of distinguishing better and worse claims through vigorous disagreement and public argument. When all of these elements are combined with one other — the notion that it is oppressed groups in particular whose group-based perspectives have been unfairly ignored or marginalised by "mainstream" political and cultural centres of power, including liberal centres of power — then the cause of sensitivity and intellectual intolerance gains powerful constituencies, and the tremendous self-confidence provided by a deep sense of historical injustice.

It is not difficult to see how this combination of views — radical multiculturalism, sensitivity and scepticism — leads to the sorts of formal and informal 'speech codes' that insist on sensitivity even at the price of 'silencing' serious discussion of such matters as affirmative action, the morality of homosexuality, and the 'naturalness' of differences between the sexes, among other things. In America the vanguard of this movement towards intellectual intolerance wrapped in the mantle of sensitivity can be found on college campuses, as David Bromwich and Jonathan Rauch have so ably explained.[36] There is, then, a real danger of a most insidious form of intolerance within the multiculturalism of mutual sensitivity.

IV. CONCLUSION: DEFENDING A LIBERAL, PLURALIST MULTICULTURALISM

I have conceded that there may be good reasons in some areas for accommodating the free exercise of religion to a greater extent than we now do. Much evidence suggests that Tocqueville was right, for example, to stress the importance of intermediate associations in a mass democracy, and religious communities are among the most active and widespread types of intermediate association, especially in America.[37] In addition, liberalism should include support for certain forms of multiculturalism.

A proper liberal civic education will insist that children learn that it is possible for fellow citizens who affirm the political supremacy of liberal values to disagree deeply about other matters: not only cultural tastes but deep religious convictions. A pluralistic multiculturalism will insist on the good of political respect for many different religions and cultures, while acknowledging the political authority of a shared point of view. Multiculturalism properly understood is an important part of a liberal civic education.

A policy of accommodation and support for multiculturalism has its place within a sensible liberalism. A liberal policy of accommodation and a pluralistic multiculturalism should not be confused with the uncritical or radical embrace of diversity. Accommodation should not aim at the 'equal' treatment of all religious beliefs and communities. We should not apologise for the fact that some communities will have a harder time than others retaining their members or convincing the young to join.

Liberal constitutionalism is not only about rights and freedom, after all, it is also about sustaining political and social structures that work to educate individuals and shape communities in ways that are congruent with liberalism. This is not only legitimate but essential political work, which will nevertheless have very unequal consequences for different religious communities.

Those with totalistic belief systems may be especially resistant to the division of our lives which is so crucial to liberalism. Those who cannot or will not distinguish their sectarian convictions about the truth as a whole from the public imperatives of citizenship in a diverse society may feel especially vulnerable and sensitive to criticism. The overweening desire to protect such sensitivities — implicit in some forms of multiculturalism — spells the end of liberalism.

My plea is that while we endeavour to make adequate room for religious practices, and while we recognise the positive contributions to our shared political life of many religious and other forms of pluralism, let us not forget or neglect the supreme importance of sustaining our shared political framework. Let us, moreover, have the honesty and tough-mindedness to acknowledge that this shared political framework — no matter how liberal and indeed because it is liberal — inevitably constrains diversity in direct and indirect ways. We should not, in particular, aim to create a level playing-field for various faith communities, and we should remember that even on a level playing-field some will lose. We will, in particular, need some fortitude in the face of those fundamentalists of all stripes who refuse ever to acknowledge the political authority of reasons, principles and a point of view above our many narrower sectarianisms.

NOTES AND REFERENCES

1. John Dewey was a good example: see his indictment of religion in *A Common Faith* (New Haven: Yale University Press, 1934).
2. In Liberal civic education and religious fundamentalism: the case of God *v.* John Rawls?, *Ethics* vol. 105 (Spring, 1995), pp. 468–496.
3. Mozert *v.* Hawkins County Bd. of Education, 827 F.2nd 1058 (6th Cir. 1987).
4. John Rawls, *Political Liberalism* (New York: Columbia University Press, 1993).
5. See Nomi Maya Stolzenberg, 'He drew a circle that shut me out': assimilation, indoctrination, and the paradox of liberal education, *Harvard Law Review*, 1992–3, vol. 106, pp. 581–667.
6. The First Amendment of the federal Constitution reads, in part, 'Congress shall make no law respecting an establishment of religion, or prohibiting the free exercise thereof'. This is one of the fundamental rights of national citizenship which, the Supreme Court has held, also applies against state governments.
7. Stephen Bates, *Battleground: one mother's crusade, the religious right, and the struggle for control of our classrooms* (New York: Poseidon, 1993), p. 314, quoting Philip H. Walkling and Chris Brannigan, Anti-sexist/anti-racist education: A possible dilemma, *Journal of Moral Education*, vol. 15 (January 1986), pp. 21–22.
8. *Ibid.*, p. 314.
9. For a representative account of the 'politics of difference', see Iris Marion Young's *Justice and the Politics of Difference* (Princeton, 1990).
10. I provide an elaborate account of all this in *Liberal Virtues: citizenship, virtue, and community in liberal constitutionalism* (Oxford: Clarendon Press, 1992).
11. Bates, *Battleground*, p. 317.
12. In this paragraph and the next, and in my account of liberalism in this paper generally, I draw on the important discussion in Rawls, *Political Liberalism, op. cit.*
13. I defend this conclusion at greater length in Liberal civic education and religious fundamentalism, *op. cit.*
14. I follow Rawls here in suggesting that we should regard reasonably disputable 'comprehensive' moral ideals—such as individuality or autonomy—as inappropriate grounds for justifying the constitutional basics in a diverse polity in the same way that religious ideals are. See *Political Liberalism, op. cit.*, pp. 35–40 and *passim*.
15. The phrase is from William Galston's Two concepts of liberalism, *Ethics*, vol. 105 (1995), pp. 516–34.
16. The phrase 'pluralistic multiculturalism' is used by Diane Ravitch for purposes related to mine, in her highly instructive argument, Multiculturalism: e pluribus plures, *American Scholar*, Summer 1990, pp. 337–354.
17. Stephen Carter, *Culture of Disbelief: how American law and politics trivialize religious devotion* (New York: Basic Books, 1993), p. 134.
18. *Ibid.*, p. 179.
19. *Ibid.*, p. 56.
20. *Ibid.*, p. 8, see also pp. 56, 63, 230.
21. *Ibid.*, pp. 26–33.
22. 410 U.S. 113 (1973).
23. Carter, *Culture of Disbelief, op. cit.*, pp. 56–66, and pp. 49–50.
24. Hackett edition, ed. James Tully, p. 33.
25. Carter often justifies religious participation in politics in public terms. When 'religious people press for a recognition in the euthanasia debate of the humanity of the person whose life might soon be ended' this is a way 'of ensuring that the tragic dimension is not lost', *Culture of Disbelief, op. cit.*, p. 249. If religious people remind us of the humanity of the terminally ill this is, once again, all to the good and entirely justifiable in terms of public reason.
26. *Ibid.*, p. 54.
27. *Ibid.*, p. 93.
28. *Ibid.*, pp. 42–43.
29. *Ibid.*, p. 94. Note also that Carter dedicates the book to his children with the wish that they 'should be able to live in a world that respects your choices instead of tolerating them'. Elsewhere he argues that 'it is

possible to maintain that crucial separation [of church and state] while treating religious beliefs with respect', p. 16, and that 'religious pluralism and equality—never mere "toleration"—should be essential parts of what makes American democracy special', p. 21.

30. *Ibid.*, p. 213. The phrase is reminiscent of some feminists' insistence on a 'women's way of knowing'.

31. See also the non-judgementalism in Young's *Politics of Difference, op. cit.*

32. Carter, *Culture of disbelief, op. cit.*, pp. 175, 230.

33. *Ibid.*, pp. 175–176.

34. See Stanley Fish, Liberalism doesn't exist, *Duke Law Journal*, vol. 1987 (December 1987), pp. 997–1001, a reply to Evolutionism, creationism, and treating religion as a hobby, *Duke Law Journal*, vol. 1987 (December 1987), pp. 977–996, an early version of a portion of Carter's book.

35. Carter, *Culture of Disbelief, op. cit.*, pp. 180–182.

36. See David Bromwich's *Politics by Other Means: higher education and group thinking* (New Haven: Yale University Press, 1992), and Jonathan Rauch's *Kindly Inquisitors* (Chicago: University of Chicago Press, 1993), both excellent treatments.

37. I discuss this evidence in Community, diversity, and civic education: toward a liberal political science of group life, *Social Philosophy and Policy*, vol. 13, no. 1, Winter 1996. For some recent evidence see Robert Putnam's *Making Democracy Work: civic traditions in modern Italy* (Princeton, 1993).

Liberalism, Education and the
Common School

TERENCE H. McLAUGHLIN

At the heart of pluralist liberal democratic societies, and the philosophical tradition of liberalism in terms of which they are frequently articulated, is the need for contrasting demands of commonality and diversity to be acknowledged and the familiar tension between them to be properly balanced. Without significant common values, principles and procedures, such societies would lack not only stability and coherence, but also the justice for their members to live together as free and equal democratic citizens. On the other hand, without principled acknowledgement of, and provision for, a scope of diversity in belief, practice and value, such societies would stand accused of inattention to the legitimate demands of pluralism and difference. The nature of these demands and the relationship between them can be variously expressed in terms of familiar tensions between universalism and particularism, the public and the non-public, and the like. It is in relation to the proper balance that should be struck between these demands that many current debates in moral and political philosophy are to be located and understood.[1]

These demands and tensions are also a central feature of conceptions of education associated with this general 'liberal democratic' perspective. They generate a two-fold educational task which can be expressed roughly as follows: On the side of commonality, education must 'transmit' the common values, principles and procedures and secure appropriate forms of respect for and allegiance to them, while on the side of diversity it must encourage appropriate forms of understanding, open-mindedness and tolerance. At least on some views, broad critical exploration of the non-public domain by pupils is urged, together with the development of their capacity to make reflective and informed decisions about significant issues in that domain. Again, it is in the examination of different aspects of the nature of, and tension between, these two tasks that much contemporary general and philosophical debate about education, particularly as it bears upon multiculturalism, is to be found.[2]

While the character of particular schooling arrangements cannot be determined solely on grounds of philosophical principle, it is widely assumed that this general conception of education yields a presumptive case in favour of common, as distinct from separate, schools. I have argued elsewhere that there is a strong case for acknowledging the compatibility of at least certain forms of separate school with the liberal democratic conception of education.[3] This case is often neglected by proponents of that conception. In this paper, however, I shall concentrate on certain questions relating to the common school. I shall argue that, while the common school is an important context in which liberal democratic educational aims can be realised, greater attention needs to be paid to complexities in the educational tasks confronting such schools which are often unacknowledged. These arise from often neglected philosophical features of liberal democratic conception of education itself.

The complexities to which I shall refer relate to the intricate relationship between the 'universalising' and 'particularising' functions of the common school, and have a bearing on the question of the extent to which such schools can be perceived as fair in their handling of value diversity.

My argument is located within the assumptions of this conception of education, central features of which will be elucidated in due course, and within the context of a pluralistic liberal democratic society. I shall not pursue wider questions arising outside these assumptions and this context, which require attention in a fuller discussion.

THE COMMON SCHOOL

The concept of the 'common school' requires clarification. A common school might be regarded as one which is open to all students regardless of differentiating characteristics such as religious, ethnic, class or cultural background. To insist that a common school is one which *actually contains* such a broad range of students is too demanding. After all, the school may in principle be open to such a range, but in practice, for various reasons, be unable to achieve it in its student body. While the actual student composition of such schools is not an insignificant matter, it seems appropriate therefore in gaining an understanding of the concept of the common school to look at the *principles* which such schools might properly espouse.

One approach to these principles is to refer to the admissions criteria which the school employs. A common school might be described as one whose admissions criteria are 'open' to a full range of students across the sorts of differentiating features referred to. However, this 'eligibility for admission' criterion is necessary but not sufficient for a common school, properly understood. A school could have an 'open' admissions policy, and indeed have a varied student body, yet not be a common school in any significant sense of the term.

That this is so is illuminated by the familiar criticism levelled at the comprehensive schools which emerged from the reorganisation of education in England and Wales in the 1960s and 1970s. While such schools had brought students of the full range of ability under the same roof, the schools faced the claim that they often lacked any coherent rationale for the provision of a common education. The complaint here was not the unrealistic one that varied students should be provided with identical educational experiences, but that a *conception* of common education was lacking.

A common school might therefore be regarded as a school which aspires not only to achieve a broad range of mix in its student body, and to offer a form of common schooling, but also one which is committed to a conception of common education.[4] How is 'a conception of common education' to be understood here?

A CONCEPTION OF COMMON EDUCATION

Within a liberal democratic framework, the notion of a conception of common education is related to the specification of a certain sort of 'educational entitlement' which is judged appropriate for all students. This 'entitlement' is seen, at least in principle, as to be secured for all. This is why the claims of (say) diversity, parental rights and the mechanisms of the educational market place, while not neglected on this perspective, are somewhat in tension with it.[5]

What are seen as 'common' to the education of all students here are the general aims, principles and 'outcomes'[6] of this 'entitlement' rather than any details of (say) institutionalisation or curriculum. This point is illuminated by Bruce Ackerman's discussion of liberal education.[7] Ackerman captures an important strand in this conception of education when he argues that it be distinguished from 'advanced horticulture' where the child is clipped like a young sapling into a preconceived pattern.[8] Rather, children must be helped in their task of 'self-definition' by being given access to a 'wide range of cultural materials' useful in the development of moral ideals and patterns of life.[9] But, for Ackerman, no 'single substantive curriculum' can be imposed on all students attending a liberal school.[10] This is because he holds that the educational aims in question can only be achieved not by a pre-planned curriculum but by educators carefully diagnosing the current values, beliefs and reactions of individual students and using such diagnoses as a basis for extending horizons. Whatever the merits of Ackerman's overall view of liberal education,[11] his discussion cautions against a temptation to argue too directly from the notion of a conception of common education to common educational provision and reminds us that the connection between a common conception of education and common schooling is at best a presumptive one.

The requirements of a common conception of education from a liberal perspective can be variously characterised. At their heart is the notion of 'an education adequate to serve the life of a free and equal citizen in any modern democracy'.[12] Central to this conception, regardless of the differences of particular theories, are the tensions between commonality and diversity which were alluded to earlier, and the educational task which they generate. Any conception of common education based on liberal principles must be alert to the dangers of basing educational influence on a form of communitarian solidarity which requires that 'children be educated to accept the singularly correct and comprehensive conception of the good life'.[13] Instead, education must seek to exert a complex two-fold influence of the sort indicated earlier. On 'common', 'universal', or 'public' matters education seeks to achieve a strong, substantial influence on the beliefs of pupils and on their wider development as persons. It is unhesitating, for example, in promoting the values of basic social morality and democratic 'civic virtue' more generally. On 'diverse', 'particular', or 'non-public' matters, education seeks to achieve a principled forebearance of influence: it seeks not to shape either the beliefs or personal qualities of pupils in the light of any substantial or 'comprehensive' conception of the good which is significantly controversial. Instead, education is either silent about such matters or encourages pupils to come to their own reflective decisions about them. One way of expressing in an overall way the nature of educational influence on this view is that is exerts a complex combination of centripetal (unifying) and centrifugal (diversifying) forces on pupils and on society itself.

The more detailed articulation of the general liberal democratic perspective gives rise to a number of prominent philosophical disputes within the framework of its general assumptions. For example, is the basic theory itself based on a substantial or 'comprehensive' conception of the good which can be justified against alternatives, or rather on a pragmatic consensus or *modus vivendi*?[14] How 'thick' and extensive are the common or 'public' values, and what is their relationship to the 'non-public' domain? What influence can the 'public' domain legitimately have over its 'non-public' counterpart? Disputes relating to such matters are reflected in differences in the varying theories of liberal education. Some of these major differences can be expressed roughly in terms of the extent to which the educational demands of commonality and diversity are interpreted maximally or minimally.[15]

With regard to commonality, minimal interpretations tend to regard the common values at stake in 'lowest common denominator' terms, and as based on 'mere' or 'de facto' consensus rather than on a consensus normatively enriched by democratic ideals, aspirations and constraints: a 'reasonable' or 'refined' consensus that *should* exist even if it contingently does not, and which is necessary to the achievement of equal respect for all. This leads to correspondingly minimal educational requirements. There is, for example, no attempt to help pupils to gain an understanding of the principles which underpin the public domain, such as those relating to 'public reason' and its scope, and little emphasis upon active aspects of democratic citizenship. More maximal interpretations see common values as enriched by democratic norms and requirements and as generating educational aims such as the development of 'democratic deliberation'[16] and Rawlsian 'reasonableness'[17] on the part of pupils, if not a more full-blown form of rational autonomy. Rawlsian 'reasonableness', for example, brings with it such educational aims as the development in pupils of a disposition to co-operate with others fairly and rationally, to ignore for 'political' purposes irrelevant particular differences of belief and identity which distinguish reasonable people and to resolve differences in mutually acceptable ways. In addition, it insists that pupils accept the Rawlsian 'burdens of judgement'[18] (the sources of ineliminable rational disagreement) and thereby obtain a grasp of the scope of reasonable diversity, and the grounds of freedom of conscience and reasonable toleration. And since liberal democratic education is concerned with more than the development of understanding, pupils are urged appropriately to employ 'public reason'[19] as well as to understand it.

On the side of diversity, minimal and maximal interpretations differ on the extent to which education is seen as having a duty to encourage pupils to gain an understanding not only of the fact of disagreement, but also of the status of the non-public domain (through, say, an appreciation of the nature of 'significant controversiality' and the proper scope of the non-public in relation to public matters). Another point on which interpretations disagree is the extent to which critical exploration of the non-public domain should be encouraged.

Although caution is needed in describing any particular theory of liberal education as 'minimal' or 'maximal' without qualification, an illustration of a generally minimal reading of at least the civic aspects of education is offered by William Galston who argues that the state has no authority to insist upon more than the development in students of 'the minimal conditions of reasonable public judgement'.[20] This does not require that pupils embrace democratic values and principles in a critically reflective way, as revealed in his insistence that, in civic education, truth and the promotion of rational enquiry should be subordinated to the aim of developing individuals who can conduct their lives within, and support, their political community. Further, on his view, pupils should not be encouraged to subject different ways of life (including those inherited from parents and local communities) to 'sceptical reflection'. In any attempt to build an ideal of wide-ranging critical reflection into the public education system, Galston accuses the state of supporting a conception of the human good 'unrelated to the functional needs of its sociopolitical institutions and at odds with the deep beliefs of many of its loyal citizens'.[21] Liberal freedom, he claims, includes the right to live an unexamined life, and the moral acceptability of 'parental bulwarks against the corrosive influence of modernist skepticism'[22] must be acknowledged.

The educational implications of John Rawls' recent work can be seen as having 'minimal' elements. In that work, Rawls seeks to confine education strictly within a 'political', as distinct from a 'comprehensive' or 'ethical', conception of liberalism.[23] Education must therefore not foster (say) autonomy and individuality as wide-ranging ideals of life as a whole, as distinct from ideals which have an important role within the political domain. Society's interest in the education of children lies 'in their role as future citizens . . . and . . . in such essential things as their acquiring the capacity to understand the public culture and to participate in its institutions, in their being economically independent and self-supporting members of society over a complete life, and in their developing the political virtues, all this from within a political point of view'.[24] Rawls concedes that these requirements may well, in effect if not in intention, lead children to develop a comprehensive liberal conception of the good, a risk which Rawls thinks must be taken, if in some cases with regret. This is because of his claim that participation in the 'overlapping consensus' which underpins public values does not involve our being hesitant or uncertain about our reasonable 'non-public' ethical beliefs.[25]

Whether liberal educational aims should be construed minimally or maximally in the sense I have described has been the subject of wide-ranging debate. It has been persuasively argued, for example by Eamonn Callan,[26] that the logic of Rawls' latest overall position frustrates Rawls' desire to restrict the intentional scope of education in the way he seeks. This is principally because, in Callan's view, the logic of Rawls' position, properly understood, requires the 'burdens of judgement' to be actively rather than passively embraced by students and to be brought to bear by them not merely on political, but also on wider, conceptions of the good. This process, together with the need to develop a political morality arising from a consensus of the appropriate kind, brings ethical liberalism and the need to develop a wide-ranging Rawlsian 'reasonableness' in 'through the back door', together with educational influence that cannot be confined to the political domain and leave 'non-public' commitments undisturbed.[27]

Notwithstanding such disputes of interpretation, a recognisable general conception of common education emerges from a broadly liberal democratic perspective which is particularly harmonious with the notion of the common school.[28]

A CONCEPTION OF COMMON EDUCATION AND COMMON SCHOOLING

As was insisted earlier, it is not possible to deduce the need for common schooling directly from a conception of common education. Nevertheless, the sort of conception of common education which has been outlined in the last section generates a strong *prima facie* case for common schooling, and this can be illustrated with reference to the demands of both commonality and diversity, whether these are construed minimally or maximally.

With regard to commonality, it is likely that the common school will be well placed to foster the shared values and sensibility needed for a stable and just democratic political and civic order, and to combat the various forces which threaten this, including social divisiveness, credal isolation and prejudice in its various forms. It may also be seen as a favourable context in which the dialogic conditions required for the development of 'democratic deliberation' and Rawlsian 'reasonableness' can flourish.

With regard to diversity, the common school may play a major role in fostering respect and understanding. A mixed environment, in which pupils confront opposing views face-to-face with those who hold them, and not merely from abstract or hypothetical sources, has much to recommend it, as does a context in which pupils associate and study together regardless of ethnic or cultural difference.

It is important to note, of course, that a common school based on a conception of common education need not eschew all forms of separateness within its walls. Claims for (say) differentiated pupil grouping or access to the curriculum can be made on various grounds within this perspective, even if they are somewhat in tension with its egalitarian and homogenising impulses.

It is also important to note that, since common schools cannot be based on an overall philosophy of life, or indeed of education, but must seek to offer a complex mixture of centripetal and centrifugal influence of the sort that has been described, parents and others may feel a lack of complete identification with them. As Amy Gutmann suggests, this may be the price that we have to pay for public institutions which treat us all as equals.[29] Common schools may therefore be supported for different reasons, including pragmatic acceptance.[30]

COMPLEXITIES IN COMMON SCHOOLING

Although the ideal of the common school in service of the liberal democratic conception of common education is attractive, the complexity of the educational responsibilities and challenges to which it gives rise is frequently underestimated. In what follows, I shall focus on complexities which have philosophical, rather than merely practical, roots.

Some philosophical difficulties experienced by liberal schooling invite wide-ranging criticisms of the liberal democratic framework of assumptions and arguments itself. For example, various critiques of liberalism of a broadly communitarian sort could be stimulated precisely by reflection on the sort of common school which the framework leads to.

However, in what follows I shall confine attention to some central complexities which arise for common schooling within the liberal democratic framework. These are general to the framework in that they arise in a significant way regardless of the particular theory or interpretation of liberal education adopted, although particular theories or interpretations provide lenses through which these complexities may be viewed.

My discussion is exploratory in character, and I shall paint the complexities I address in broad brush strokes. This involves the use of terminology in a rather loose way. I shall appeal, for example, to a rough distinction between the public and the non-public[31] which requires much more detailed treatment in a fuller account.

Context, Neutrality and Substantiality

Common schools aspiring to offer a conception of common education within a liberal democratic frame of reference exist in social, cultural and political contexts which are complex and changing. If it is accepted that a distinction between the public and the non-public domain is broadly tenable[32] it is important to note that what is in fact regarded as significantly controversial, and therefore as a public or a non-public matter, will vary in different contexts. Nor is this simply a matter of given societies being imperfectly liberal: the theoretical resources of liberalism are not precise enough to produce definitive answers to such questions. Further, just as nations and states cannot be culturally neutral, neither can the common schools located within them, even though they may for liberal reasons be uneasy with particularities. The fact that the common school must have a 'cultural content' and therefore cannot offer a culture-neutral environment is reinforced by noting the close historical relationship between civic education and national education.[33]

The cultural neutrality or otherwise of the common school is illuminated by Michael Walzer's distinction between Liberalism 1 and Liberalism 2. This distinction, developed in relation to Charles Taylor's discussion of the politics of recognition, refers to liberal states, but can be applied to public institutions.[34] Liberalism 1 is, in virtue of its strong commitment to individual rights, committed also to a 'rigorously neutral state'—'a state without cultural or religious projects or, indeed, any sort of collective goals beyond the personal freedom and the physical security, welfare and safety of its citizens'.[35] In contrast, Liberalism 2 provides for a state 'committed to the survival and flourishing of a particular nation, culture, or religions, . . . so long as the basic rights of citizens who have different commitments or no such commitments at all are protected'.[36] Walzer comments that liberals can consistently choose either kind of liberalism according to particular circumstances. Liberalism 1, for example, is appropriate in immigrant countries such as the United States, where instead of a nation state, there is a 'nation of nationalities', and (say) a separation of church and state is called for. But such a decision is not governed by an absolute commitment to neutrality or a distrust of particularist identities, but rather by 'the social condition and the actual life choices of *these* men and women'.[37] In Liberalism 2, nation states are non-neutral with regard to the cultural survival of the majority nation, but liberal principles are satisfied by a 'strong theory of rights'.[38] Such a choice, suggests Walzer, is appropriate in countries such as Norway, where there is a long-established majority nation. So long as basic rights are respected, there is no requirement for equal provision or equal protection of minority cultures. Amy Gutmann suggests that Liberalism 1 and 2, rather than being seen as contrasting conceptions of liberalism as a whole, should be seen as options for particular realms within a liberal society. In some realms Liberalism 1 is appropriate, in others (given satisfaction of basic rights) Liberalism 2.

This distinction between kinds of liberalism is of significance because, when applied (albeit roughly) to the common school, it illuminates the point that, in any given context, the character of the common school cannot be read in detail directly from liberal principles alone, but must be forged in, and be supported by, a debate and consensus about the cultural basis on which its work proceeds. If aspiring to base its work on a form of Liberalism 1, the common school faces a debate about precisely what are to count as appropriate forms of neutrality, and whether indeed any wide-ranging neutrality is either feasible or desirable in a properly educational institution.[39] Amy Gutmann notes that in the United States local communities have been given the democratic right to shape their schools in their own cultural image in the manner of Liberalism 2, within principled liberal democratic constraints. These require such schools, as part of the satisfaction of the 'basic rights' referred to earlier, to be nonrepressive, nondiscriminatory and deliberative[40] and so to satisfy essential democratic principles. But within these limits the shared beliefs and cultural practices which are particular to communities can be transmitted and maintained.

Whether based on Liberalism 1 or 2, common schools are therefore confronted by the need for a wide-ranging debate about what are to be regarded as the cultural norms to be presented to pupils. This has a bearing on the role of religion in common schools, which is a frequent source of controversy. In the light of Walzer's distinctions, there can be no context-free way of determining this matter. In some situations, an approach based on a form of Liberalism 1 would seem to be appropriate, with either silence about religion or an attempt at appropriate forms of study of it which do not presuppose the truth of any particular creed. Liberalism 2 would seem to permit in certain circumstances (for example, in contexts where there is little religious diversity, no separation of church and state and a national religion) the presentation of that religion, at least in its cultural manifestations, as normative within the common school. Given the need for Liberalism 2 to preserve basic rights, expressed perhaps in a commitment to a principle such as 'non-repression', this should stop short of the sort of substantial religious formation that might take place in a religious school. Rather, religion is seen as part of an initial culture which is given to pupils. To satisfy liberal principles, such a conception of common schooling must not inhibit critical reflection on this initial culture, and indeed must encourage it. But the demands of (say) the

Rawlsian 'burdens of judgement' may not require neutrality about religion from the outset.[41] The postwar approach to religious education and religious worship adopted in common schools in England and Wales,[42] suitably enriched by a critical dimension, seems to be roughly compatible with this line of argument. Given a similar enrichment, this may be true also of recent proposals from the Islamic Academy that, since survey evidence suggests that most people in England and Wales believe in God, a form of theistic belief shared by the major religions in the country should be made the normative basis of the common school. By implication, agnostics and atheists in such schools, though able to articulate their perspective against this norm, should, if unhappy, seek separate schools.[43]

A democratic decision in favour of such a policy which is made in the light of appropriate democratic constraints and not merely on a form of majoritarianism,[44] and which acknowledges the need to satisfy the demands of non-repression and the like, may not infringe liberal principles. However, it is likely to be appropriate only in very homogenous societies and communities. The continuing debates in England and Wales about the role of religion in common schools and the precise meaning to be given to the recently introduced requirement that the 'spiritual development' of pupils be promoted and inspected[45] indicates that such conditions do not obtain to any great extent here. Answers to survey questions do not provide a reliable guide to the substantial religious beliefs of the population as a whole, or to their views on the role that the common school should play with regard to religion.

The common school has an obligation to 'transmit' the basic or non-negotiable norms which articulate the framework of a liberal democratic society. In addition to these, the common school cannot avoid transmitting some norms which are culturally distinctive in the sense that they selectively favour some beliefs, practices and values in ways that go beyond what could be justified from a strictly neutral point of view. In the light of the line of argument sketched above, these might be regarded as 'default' norms in the sense that they are part of an initial culture which is open to criticism and challenge: what is 'taken for granted', as a starting point. Whilst they are culturally specific they do not constrain reflection. However, since what is 'taken for granted', even in a preliminary way, is often particularly sensitive in relation to matters on which there is significant disagreement, particular care needs to be taken in reviewing and determining these norms. This is particularly so concerning matters on which members of 'minority traditions' may feel that their own perspectives are insufficiently recognised and valued, as distinct from merely tolerated.[46]

Common schools cannot ignore views of this kind and public opinion more generally (including the views of parents) even if, on liberal principles, they might want in some cases to extend and develop them. In controversial matters, therefore, such schools face the task of working out in concrete terms how to proceed in a way which combines as far as possible broad acceptability to public opinion with conformity to liberal principles. Schools need help in this from a wide-ranging debate within the societies in which they are located, which seeks to address the issues clearly and achieve consensus about practical strategies and approaches for the handling of controversial issues. It is in the context of such a debate that such vexed matters as the relationship between moral and religious education[47] and the appropriate thickness of civic education[48] can be addressed. The scope for the achievement of consensus in such a debate should not be underestimated. Without it, schools approach their work undersupported by the democratic society they seek to serve.

The scope of the public

Common schools have an obligation to ensure that pupils not only become committed to the 'public' values, but that they also become aware of their proper character, and, in particular, their scope. The public values, however robustly conceived, cover a part, and not the whole, of the moral life, a point which Rawls has been at pains to stress in his later work. There are a number of implications of this for the work of the common school.

The school must clearly indicate the limited scope of the 'public' values. Whether a given action should be accepted or tolerated within the public or civic domain and be legal does not *ipso facto* make that action fully acceptable morally from all points of view, and education must make this clear. While the salience of public values for political purposes must be insisted upon by any common school operating within a liberal democratic framework, the logic of that framework requires that it be made clear to pupils that 'public evaluation' is conducted in a morally. circumscribed language and that wider moral perspectives exist from which fuller moral appraisal is possible and necessary. A failure to clarify this point may lead to pupils gaining a distorted perception of the moral life. While it is true that liberal values have unavoidable implications for values held in the 'non-public' domain,[49] the school has a principled responsibility to try to avoid giving illicit salience to 'public' matters and underplaying the role that reasonable moral views in the 'non-public' domain play in overall moral evaluation. Thus, for example, although the school must make it clear that controversial religious considerations should not have decisive weight in the public domain, the school should not seek to promote a secular view of life as a whole.[50]

The school therefore has the task of developing in pupils a kind of 'moral bilingualism'[51] and its related consciousness, capable of distinguishing between, on the one hand, the demands of civic virtue and, on the other, virtue seen from a fuller perspective. This presents common schools with a number of complex tasks.

Pupils must be provided with proper understanding of what is involved in giving 'respect' to differing views. Democratic mutual respect for reasonable differences of moral view requires more than a grudging attitude of 'live and let live'. In the light, for example, of acceptance of the Rawlsian 'burdens of judgement', reasonable differences are to be judged as in some sense within the civic moral pale, and this enriches respect, and indeed toleration, with principle. But such respect and toleration does not necessarily require that disagreement and disapproval concerning the substantive value differences be dissolved. Our disagreements and disapprovals, often arising from our differing 'comprehensive' theories of the good, persist and should not be smoothed away,[52] and this is true even if a very strong interpretation of the implications of viewing others with whom we disagree as *mistaken* is avoided.[53] While it is true that, within a liberal democratic framework, the character and scope of our disagreements are narrowed (often, for example, being confined to the non-public sphere) and refined (say, by the acknowledgement of the deep-seated nature of controversy) they nevertheless remain. The common school must therefore achieve the right kind of openness to diversity on the part of pupils and avoid blurring the distinction in their minds between according differing views 'civic respect' and giving them unqualified approval, perhaps on a relativistic basis.

An interesting illustration of the complexities which arise concerning these requirements is to be found in Patricia White's recent discussion of the educational treatment of homosexuality.[54] Liberal educational principles demand that this not be ignored as an educational issue, but the values which should be brought to bear on its treatment repay attention. In her discussion of whether homosexuality is morally wrong, White considers only whether such relationships violate the basic principles which relate to life in a democratic society. Having concluded that they do not, she draws the conclusion that the school should not only present homosexuality as a morally acceptable lifestyle which pupils might adopt, but should also contribute to its flourishing.

This approach seems to go too far. Strong liberal arguments may support the moral acceptability, for political purposes, of homosexuality within the sphere of 'civic virtue'. In arguing that the school should present homosexuality as a morally acceptable lifestyle and should help it to flourish, White may be referring only to the civic sphere, and claiming that the moral influence of the school should be confined strictly to 'public' values. This general claim about the moral influence of the school will be discussed in the next section. However, it seems more likely that White is arguing that the common school should present homosexuality as morally acceptable in a more wide-ranging way. This position depends on the claim that there cannot be any reasonable 'non-public' moral criticism of homosexuality, which in turn depends upon judgements about the current state of reasonable non-public moral opinion on this topic. Without entering into further detailed discussion of this particular example, we can note that it illustrates the need of the common school to distinguish in any particular moral issue between what is (a) fully morally acceptable both from a civic perspective and from any reasonable non-public perspective and (b) what is morally acceptable from a civic perspective but, from at least some reasonable non-public perspectives, not fully. This brings with it the difficulty in determining what is to count as a *reasonable* non-public evaluation of a particular matter.

Such matters cannot be determined in a wholly abstract way, and need to be included in the wide-ranging debate called for in the last section.

Any attempt to develop a 'moral bilingualism' in pupils confronts the difficulty of potential conflict between securing appropriate forms of public respect for (say) forms of lifestyle while illuminating the fact that from some reasonable non-public perspectives those lifestyles are seen as morally reprehensible.

Liberalism introduces a division into our lives, and into our experience of others, a point well captured in the remark that in a liberal democratic society we confront strangers as well as friends. Judith Shklar has drawn attention to the complexity of the ethical difficulties, attitudes and virtues that liberalism demands, not least the role that certain forms of hypocrisy play in sustaining a liberal democratic society.[55] They generate a set of complex demands on both teachers and pupils.

It should be noted that these problems remain whether or not the school is seen as having a very extensive role in relation to non-public matters. They arise simply from the school having a role in articulating the character of the public virtues. This cannot be fulfilled without reference to the 'non-public'. The sort of reference that is appropriate will be addressed in the next section.

Addressing the non-public

As was indicated earlier, conceptions of common education vary according to the extent to which it is thought appropriate for the common school to enter into the 'non-public' domain.

At the most minimal level, the school may maintain on these matters what Kenneth Strike refers to as 'liberal silence'.[56] The inadequacies of such an approach are wide-ranging, and have force even on the sorts of minimal view of liberal education outlined earlier. It is hard to see how the task of making pupils aware of the nature and scope of the public values can be accomplished to any great extent without attention to the non-public. This is particularly so if the 'public' values are seen as constructed not from a form of 'grounded liberalism' but from an 'overlapping consensus' of non-public views; a consensus that might be explored at school level through a 'hermeneutical dialogue' between the 'primary moral languages' of pupils.[57] In the absence of such a dialogue the 'common culture' of society may become unduly thin. Such an exploration of the 'non-public' would also seem to be demanded by the need to develop an understanding of the nature of morality even based on a more pragmatic *'modus vivendi'* view of consensus,[58] and the 'burdens of judgement' can only be understood in relation to the non-public matters on which they are brought to bear. Further, given that the distinction between what is to count as a 'public' and a 'non-public' matter is itself a matter for controversy, a debate at school level about this issue cannot be avoided. The common school should therefore not neglect its particularising functions in favour of its universalising ones.[59]

A powerful argument for the involvement of the common school with the non-public domain arises from the need for the development in pupils of imaginative engagement, understanding and sympathy with views with which they disagree. Silence about the 'non-public' domain is not neutral in effect and is also likely to disfavour cultural minorities, whose own distinctive moral perspectives may therefore fail to receive attention. Indeed, such silence might itself constitute, in effect if not in intention, a form of repression.[60] The aim of helping pupils to become 'morally bilingual' also requires connections to be made between 'public' moral language and the 'non-public' moral language of pupils if they are not to become schizophrenic.[61] Further, the absence from the common school of wide-ranging substantial moral debate could scarcely be a good preparation for democracy.

Given that the common school should play some attention to the non-public domain, disagreements arise over the degree of critical reflection that should be promoted with regard to it, together with the question of the perspective from which criticism should take place. Macedo, for example, holds that the Rawlsian 'burdens of judgement' are best seen as an accessory to a civic education which sets 'non-public' matters aside. It is wrong for the school to encourage pupils to (say) subject the religious beliefs of their parents to sceptical investigation.[62] But even if the work of the school is confined to the aim of illuminating rather than criticising views in the non-public domain, a number of major requirements come into focus.

One requirement would seem to be that non-public perspectives should not be excluded from the discussion of moral issues. To return to the earlier example of the educational treatment of homosexuality, Patricia White acknowledges that religious views on this subject should be treated as part of a study of the religions in question. However, these views need to be brought to bear on discussions about a 'morally acceptable lifestyle' if a full understanding of this is to be developed. This is true also in areas such as Personal and Social Education, where 'public' and 'non-public' considerations of value are closely interrelated. The moral aspects of sex education more generally are particularly liable to be treated in terms only of the public values.[63] Both 'public' and 'non-public' perspectives must be brought to bear on moral issues discussed by pupils if they are to be properly and fully understood. Although in a pluralist society it may be judged that religious perspectives should not provide the ultimate criterion of moral rectitude, such perspectives should not be excluded from the discussion of moral issues.[64] There is no suggestion therefore that 'non-public' perspectives should be presented as having the same force as 'public' considerations, but rather that they should be illuminated for consideration. Such a policy may be particularly welcome to some members of cultural minority groups, who feel that a *de facto* secularist interpretation of moral issues is being imposed on their children. What they often seek is not a privileging of their own value positions, but that the common school should live up to its own principles in a more sustained way by including an appropriate range of moral perspectives on prominent issues.

As well as ensuring that these groups are not excluded from the discussion of moral issues, the common school must illuminate non-public views fairly and without preconceptions. One danger which the common school must avoid is that of promoting a relativist view of such values. The view that certain issues are significantly controversial, and that they ultimately require assessment by individuals, is importantly distinct from an acceptance of relativism. Beyond noting that reasonable 'non-public' values are significantly controversial, liberalism is silent about their truth and falsity. Another respect in which the common school can distort 'non-public' values is by viewing them through the lens of an illicitly comprehensive liberalism, and in a unduly context-free way. Such dangers are particularly apparent in relation to religion, and in the fair presentation of more traditional forms of religious belief.[65]

These tasks are confronted by many difficulties, not least the potential conflict between the civic and illuminative aims which were noted in the last section. One difficulty concerns the determination of the scope of the range of (reasonable) non-public views to be considered in relation to given matters. Another problem concerns that of 'bringing to life' in a genuinely illuminating way 'non-public' forms of life, where once again religion is a prominent example of difficulty.[66]

Another problem is that although the school is not in principle committed to a crude form of general neutrality about moral values, in practice the attitude enjoined on teachers in relation to matters in the 'non-public' domain may well carry over into the moral influence of the school as a whole, weakening it. Teachers may develop a general reluctance to exert moral influence, whether by precept or example, particularly if there is uncertainty about where in practice the line is to be drawn between public and non-public values, or if a wide-ranging relativism gets a foothold. This problem can be expressed more specifically in terms of the moral example which the teacher should give.[67]

CONCLUSIONS

The responsibilities of the common school which have emerged from this discussion render it a complex institution. It might be wondered whether these responsibilities are too difficult, or perhaps impossible, to discharge. Macedo, for example, notes that the Rawlsian 'burdens of judgement' are very complex and could only be understood by very advanced students.[68] Further, it might be wondered how far the project of illuminating other ways of life and perspectives in the 'non-public' domain can really be successful, and how coherent it is to attempt to develop the 'moral bilingualism' that has been referred to. In the light of this it might be argued that the best that the common school can hope to do is to 'transmit' the public values and run the risk of developing in pupils a *de facto* acceptance of 'comprehensive' liberalism.

A number of other prominent difficulties arise for the common school, not least those relating to the justificatory basis it can invoke, given the critiques of postmodernism[69] and the abandonment of earlier epistemological grounds on which its work has been based.[70]

Wide-ranging worries of the kind indicated lead to calls for the diversification of schools along philosophical, ideological and religious lines, and not only from those who invoke familiar religious grounds.[71]

The common school remains an attractive ideal. It is, however, a complex one. Its vindication depends precisely on the willingness and ability of common schools to address this complexity.

NOTES AND REFERENCES

1. See, for example, Rawls, J. (1993) *Political Liberalism* (New York, Columbia University Press); Taylor, C. (1992) *Multiculturalism and 'The Politics of Recognition'* (Princeton, NJ, Princeton University Press); Milligan, D. and Watts Miller, W. (1992) (Eds) *Liberalism, Citizenship and Autonomy* (Aldershot, Avebury).
2. See, for example, Gutmann, A. (1987) *Democratic Education* (Princeton, NJ, Princeton University Press), esp. pp. 41–47: Leicester, M. and Taylor, M. (Eds) (1992) *Ethics, Ethnicity and Education* (London, Kogan Page).
3. McLaughlin, T. H. (1987) 'Education for all' and religious schools in: Haydon, G. (Ed) *Education for a Pluralist Society. Philosophical Perspectives on the Swann Report* Bedford Way Papers No. 30 (London,

Institute of Education, University of London); McLaughlin, T. H. (1992a) 'The ethics of separate schools', in: Leicester, M. and Taylor, M. (Eds), *op. cit.*

4. For the distinction between 'common schooling' and 'a conception of common education' I am indebted to Eamonn Callan. See Callan, E. (1995) Common schools for common education, *Canadian Journal of Education* (forthcoming).

5. On parental rights see McLaughlin, T. H. (1994a) The scope of parents' educational rights, in: Halstead, J. M. (Ed) *Parental Choice and Education. Principles, Policy and Practice* (London, Kogan Page). On the mechanisms of the educational market place see McLaughlin, T. H. (1994b) Politics, markets and schools: the central issues, in: Bridges, D. and McLaughlin, T. H. (Eds) *Education and the Market Place* (London, The Falmer Press).

6. It is important, of course, to note that since liberal education includes such aims as the development of 'critically independent judgement' what counts as an 'outcome' on this view should not be understood in too restricted a way.

7. Ackerman, B. (1980) *Social Justice in the Liberal State* (New Haven & London, Yale University Press), Ch. 5.

8. *Ibid.*, p. 149.

9. *Ibid.*, pp. 155–156.

10. *Ibid.*, p. 156.

11. For criticisms of Ackerman's position see, for example, Crittenden, B. (1988) *Parents, the State and the Right to Educate* (Victoria, Melbourne University Press), pp. 139–154.

12. Gutmann, A. (1992) Introduction, in: Taylor, C. (1992), *op. cit.*, p. 14.

13. Gutmann, A. (1993) Democracy and democratic education, *Studies in Philosophy and Education*, 12, 1, p. 3.

14. For a relevant distinction between 'grounded' and 'pragmatic' liberalism see Strike, K. A. (1994) On the construction of public speech: pluralism and public reason, *Educational Theory*, 44, 1, pp. 1–26.

15. For a related discussion concerning education for citizenship see McLaughlin, T. H. (1992b) Citizenship, diversity and education: a philosophical perspective, *Journal of Moral Education*, 21, 3, pp. 235–250.

16. Gutmann, A. (1987), *op. cit.*, pp. 50–52.

17. Rawls, J. (1993) *op. cit.*, pp. 48–54.

18. Rawls, J. (1993), *op. cit.*, pp. 54–58.

19. On these issues see, for example, Callan, E. (1995), *op. cit.*, On the notion of 'public speech' and its educational implications see, for example, Strike, K. A. (1994), *op. cit.*

20. Galston, W. (1989) Civic education in the liberal state, in: Rosenblum, N. (Ed) *Liberalism and the Moral Life* (Cambridge MA, Harvard University Press), p. 99.

21. *Ibid.*, p. 100.

22. *Ibid.*

23. On this distinction see Rawls, J. (1993), *op. cit.*, esp. Ch. 1 and pp. 154–158.

24. *Ibid.*, p. 200.

25. *Ibid.*, p. 63.

26. Callan, E. (1994a) Political liberalism and political education. Paper presented to the Cambridge Branch of the Philosophy of Education Society of Great Britain, April.

27. For Stephen Macedo's disagreement with Callan on this interpretation of Rawls and on the matters at stake see Macedo, S. (1995) Liberal civic education and its limits: a comment on Eamonn Callan, *Canadian Journal of Education* (forthcoming). Compare Strike, K. A. (1994), *op. cit.*

28. For general statements of this perspective on education see, for example, Gutmann, A. (1987), *op. cit.*; White J. (1990) *Education and the Good Life: Beyond the National Curriculum* (London, Kogan Page). On pluralism and its educational implications see, for example, Crittenden, B. (1982) *Cultural Pluralism and Common Curriculum* (Melbourne, Melbourne University Press) and Crittenden, B. (1988), *op. cit.*, esp. Chs. 5, 7. On multiculturalism and liberal education see Gewirth, A. (1994) The moral basis of liberal education, *Studies in Philosophy and Education*, 13, 2, pp. 111–124.

29. Gutmann, A. (1992), *op. cit.*, p. 4.

30. See, for example, Cooling, T. (1994) *A Christian Vision for State Education: Reflections on the Theology of Education* (London, SPCK).

31. On the inadequacy of any one-dimensional distinction between the public and the private realm to determine decisions about whether sex education or religious education should take place in common schools see Gutmann, A. (1987), pp. 107–115; 123–125.

32. On the indispensibility of such a distinction from a liberal point of view, despite difficulties in specifying its exact character, see, for example, Shklar, J. (1991) The liberalism of fear, in: Rosenblum, N. (Ed), *op. cit.*

33. On this matter see Tamir, Y. (1993) United we stand? The educational implications of the politics of difference, *Studies in Philosophy and Education*, 12, 1, pp. 57–70.

34. Walzer, M. (1992) Comment, in: Taylor, C. *op. cit.*

35. *Ibid.*, p. 99.

36. *Ibid.*

37. *Ibid.*, p. 103 (emphasis in original).

38. Thus Walzer suggests that states committed to Liberalism 2 can vindicate their Liberalism by 'tolerating and respecting ethnic and religious differences and allowing all minorities an equal freedom to organize their members, express their cultural values, and reproduce their way of life in civil society and in the family', Walzer, M. (1992), *op. cit.*, p. 100. Compare Gutmann, A. (1992), *op. cit.*, pp. 10–11.

39. On this see, for example, Gutmann, A. (1987), *op. cit.*, pp. 33–41; 54–56.

40. Gutmann, A. (1992), *op. cit.*, p. 12. Compare Gutmann, A. (1987), *op. cit.*, 41–47; 71–75.

41. On the relationship between moral and religious education in common schools see Gutmann, A. (1987), *op. cit.*, pp. 123–125.

42. I refer loosely to the approach adopted to these matters until (roughly) the 1960s. This assumed the truth of a general form of Christianity and the role of the common school in transmitting it. See Hull, J. (1984) *Studies in Religion and Education* (London, The Falmer Press), esp. Ch. 3.

43. The Islamic Academy (1990) *Faith as the Basis of Education in a Multi-Faith Multi-Cultural Country* (Cambridge, The Islamic Academy).

44. See Gutmann, A. (1987), Ch. 4.

45. White, J. (1994) Instead of OFSTED: a critical discussion of OFSTED on 'Spiritual, Moral, Social and Cultural Development', *Cambridge Journal of Education*, 24, 3, pp. 369–377; Carr, D. (1995) Towards a distinctive conception of spiritual education, *Oxford Review of Education* 21.1, pp. 83–98, See also Jackson, R. (1992) The misrepresentation of religious education, in: Leicester, M. and Taylor, M. (Eds) *op. cit.*

46. On the question of recognition see, for example, Taylor, C. (1992), *op. cit.*

47. On this see, for example, Callan, E. (1989) Godless moral education and liberal tolerance, *Journal of Philosophy of Education*, 23, 2, pp. 267–281.

48. Callan, E. (1994b) Beyond sentimental civic education, *American Journal of Education*, 102, pp. 190–221.

49. Macedo, S. (1990) *Liberal Virtues: Citizenship, Virtue and Community in Liberal Constitutionalism* (Oxford, Clarendon Press): 'Liberalism provides wide bounds within which people are free to settle their own religious beliefs, aesthetic values, and so on. And yet, basic liberal principles (of respect for persons and their rights, for example) wash across and seep into the whole of our lives, not determining all our choices but limiting them all and structuring and conditioning our lives as a whole. Illiberal forms of private association are strictly ruled out. Many other interests and commitments, whilst not strictly ruled out, are bound to be discouraged by the free, open, pluralistic, progressive, and (arguably) commercialistic nature of a liberal society' (p. 54). On the implications for 'non-public' beliefs arising from assuming the Rawlsian 'burdens of judgement' see Callan, E. (1994a), *op. cit.*

50. On the relationship between religion and education, see, for example, Ashraf. S. A. and Hirst, P. H. (1994) (Eds) *Religion and Education: Islamic and Christian Approaches* (Cambridge, The Islamic Academy); Haydon, G. (1994) Conceptions of the secular in society, polity and schools, *Journal of Philosophy of Education*, 28, 1, pp. 65–75.

51. Strike, K. A. (1993) Ethical discourse and pluralism, in: Strike, K. A. and Lance Ternasky, P. (Eds) *Ethics for Professionals in Education: Perspectives for Preparation and Practice* (New York, Teachers College Press), Ch. 12.

52. See Macedo, S. (1995), *op. cit.*

53. Gardner, P. (1992) Propositional attitudes and multicultural education or believing others are mistaken, in: Horton, J. and Nicholson, P. (Eds) *Toleration: Philosophy and Practice* (Aldershot, Avebury).

54. White, P. (1991) Parents' rights, homosexuality and education, *British Journal of Educational Studies*, XXXIX, 4, pp. 398–408.

55. Shklar, J. (1984) *Ordinary Vices* (Cambridge MA, Belknap Press of Harvard University Press), esp. Chs. 2, 6.

56. Strike, K. A. (1993), *op. cit.*, p. 178.

57. Strike, K. A. (1994), *op. cit.*

58. Haydon, G. (1995) Thick or thin? The cognitive content of moral education in a plural democracy, *Journal of Moral Education*, 24, 1, pp. 53–64. See also Haydon, G. (1994), *op. cit.*
59. Strike, K. A. (1994), *op. cit.*
60. Amy Gutmann claims that non-repression in schooling 'prohibits educational authorities from shielding students from reasonable (not correct or uncontroversial) political views represented by the adult citizenry or from censoring reasonable challenges to those views', Gutmann, A. (1987), *op. cit.*, p. 98.
61. Strike, K. A. (1993), *op. cit.*, pp. 182–183.
62. Macedo, S. (1985), *op. cit.*
63. For a discussion of the varying moral perspectives that might appropriately be brought to bear in sex education see Health Education Authority (1994) *Sex Education, Values and Morality* (London, Health Education Authority).
64. On these matters see, for example, Haydon, G. (1994), *op. cit.*
65. Cooling, T. (1994), *op. cit.*
66. On this matter see, for example, McLaughlin, T. H. (1995) Wittgenstein, education and religion, in: Smeyers, P. and Marshall, J. (Eds) *Philosophy and Education: Accepting Wittgenstein's Challenge* (Dordrecht, Kluwer).
67. On this matter see Carr, D. (1993) Moral values and the teacher: beyond the paternal and the permissive, *Journal of Philosophy of Education*, 27, 2, pp. 193–207.
68. Macedo, S. (1995), *op. cit.*
69. On this see, for example, Carr, W. (1995) Education and democracy: confronting the postmodernist challenge. *Journal of Philosophy of Education*, 29.1, pp. 75–91.
70. Hirst, P. H. (1993) Education, knowledge and practices, in: Barrow, R. and White, P. (Eds) *Beyond Liberal Education. Essays in honour of Paul H. Hirst*, (London, Routledge). Compare Hirst, P. H. (1985) Education and diversity of belief, in: Felderhof, M. C. (Ed) *Religious Education in a Pluralistic Society* (London, Hodder & Stoughton).
71. Hargreaves, D. (1994) *The Mosaic of Learning: Schools and Teachers for the Next Century* (London, Demos), pp. 18–22.

Voluntary Apartheid? Problems of Schooling for Religious and Other Minorities in Democratic Societies

MARK HALSTEAD

It is sometimes claimed that certain ways of life systematically lose out in Western liberal democratic societies, particularly in terms of members being required to surrender any real chance of passing on their cultural heritage and most cherished values to their children in an uncompromised form. Typically, such ways of life belong to homogeneous and relatively self-contained subgroups which do not fully share the liberal framework of values. There has been considerable philosophical interest in such subgroups in recent years, and in the question of whether they may justifiably seek a differentiated form of schooling for their children in order to preserve their cultural identity from being unduly influenced and thereby significantly diluted by the majority.

This paper initially distinguishes between political and cultural communities and proceeds to identify the different kinds of cultural minority which may be anxious to preserve their distinctive identity from the undue influence of dominant groups in society. Religious minorities are distinguished from other groups in terms both of composition and of aspirations. Philosophers looking at religious minorities from the outside have traditionally been interested in assessing how far they fall short of liberal ideals, but by reversing this process and looking at liberalism, and in particular liberal education, from the outside — as if through the eyes of someone with an overriding religious commitment — I hope to generate fresh insights on what it is like for religious minorities to live in a liberal society. Finally, the possibility is explored of a compromise which would generate an equality of dignity and respect for religious minorities, enabling them to retain their specific cultural identity and preserve this across the generations, while at the same time allowing them to participate fully as citizens of a democratic society.

CULTURAL COMMUNITIES AND THE STATE

An initial distinction must be made between two kinds of community, the political and the cultural. The political community, at least in its liberal democratic version, is a community of citizens who owe an equal duty of loyalty to the constitutional government and who are, in turn, accorded equal rights and fundamental liberties without regard to race, ethnicity, religion, gender, mother tongue or any other irrelevant consideration. The rights and liberties upheld by the state typically include the right to life and liberty, the right to vote and to hold public office, the right to due process of law, the right to freedom of conscience and the free expression of religion, and the right to health care and education. The cultural community, on the other hand, is a community of people who believe they share an identity and a sense of belonging and loyalty as a result of holding in common, and valuing the distinctiveness of, at least one (and normally several) of the following characteristics: language, religion, ethnicity, history and tradition. In fact, two other items can be added to this list — nationality and race — because there are compelling arguments that these should be considered cultural or ideological phenomena rather than biologically determined groupings.[1]

The distinction between political and cultural communities is maintained most clearly where the state adopts a position of neutrality with regard to cultural groups and their collective goals but strongly protects the rights of its citizens as individuals. Walzer[2] calls this approach to government 'Liberalism 1', and he contrasts it with an approach in which the state extends its area of concern to the cultural character of the community and enacts laws designed to preserve its distinctive cultural, linguistic or religious heritage ('Liberalism 2'). 'Liberalism 1' can be seen at its clearest in the American doctrine of the separation of church and state, whereby the state consciously avoids the entanglement of its own institutions (including the public school) with any particular religious tradition. 'Liberalism 2', on the other hand, may be seen in the action of the French government which recently passed a bill through parliament stating that French is the 'only legal language in France', or in the current German policy of offering full citizenship to inhabitants of Russia or other parts of Eastern Europe so long as some ancestral link connecting them with Germany can be established, but denying it to (or at least making it very difficult for) even second- or third-generation 'resident foreigners' such as the Turkish community in Germany.[3] In this case, membership of the political community is conferred on the basis of membership of the cultural community (the German nation). 'Liberalism 2' does not necessarily imply that the political community coincides completely with the cultural community, in the sense that *all* citizens are of the same nationality or share a single language or religion; but it does require that where the state aligns itself with the nation, culture or religion of the majority, the basic rights of citizens with other loyalties and commitments should be respected.

Some basic rights, such as the right to vote, belong exclusively to the political domain, whereas others may be tinged to a greater or lesser extent with cultural considerations, and in some cases the intertwining of cultural and political considerations seems virtually inevitable. For example, the right to education can never be exercised in a cultural vacuum. Therefore the debate about education and culture is not so much about *whether* cultural influences occupy a justifiable place in schools, as about the *kinds* of cultural influences which are justifiable. Indeed it may be argued that a sense of belonging to a clear cultural group is an essential part of the security and guidance that children need as they develop gradually towards maturity and personal autonomy. 'Liberalism 1', because of its insistence on the non-involvement of the state in any particular cultural tradition, has some difficulties here. Two possibilities emerge. One is to develop an enriched concept of citizenship which includes some features typical of cultural communities. This is exactly what American 'civil religion' is about, with its festivals (Thanksgiving), its rituals (saluting the flag), its sacred texts (the Gettysburg Address) and its prophets (Martin Luther King). The other possibility is to develop a self-conscious multiculturalism based on an equality of respect and recognition for a wide variety of different cultures. There is a sense in which, even if pluralist states did not exist in the modern world, multicultural education would have to be invented in order to satisfy the need for liberals to introduce the notion of culture impartially to children. 'Liberalism 2', on the other hand, has no such difficulties. Where the state is committed to the survival and flourishing of a particular nation, the cultural values of that nation automatically provide the context in which children grow up. However, this approach does not lend itself as readily to the cultural pluralism which typifies most present-day Western liberal democratic states. Where cultural pluralism prevails, the provision of a secure cultural context for all citizens equally may become much more problematic, particularly in the area of education. Walzer[4] implies that in 'Liberalism 2' the state might be committed to the survival and flourishing of more than one nation, culture or religion at the same time, but this may apply only to societies which are pluralist in the sense that no single cultural group forms a majority within the state. In the more common sense of cultural pluralism, where the people of one or more cultural minorities live alongside those of the cultural majority, it is clear that to recognise a multiplicity of cultures would, of course, reduce the strength of the connection between the state and the majority cultural community. The French government could not rule that French was the only legal language in France while at the same time offering public support to schools where pupils were taught in Breton or Arabic.

Although much more needs to be said to articulate fully the arguments being developed here, I hope that the basic distinctions are clear enough. Several questions now emerge. If we grant that culture-free education is impossible, does 'Liberalism 1' or 'Liberalism 2' provide the more justifiable framework of values for education in a culturally pluralist society? Which is more acceptable to minority cultural communities? And are these two the only possible approaches within the framework of a liberal democracy? Before these questions can be considered, the concept of pluralism must be examined more closely.

PLURALIST STATES AND THE RECOGNITION
OF CULTURAL MINORITIES

It is widely assumed[5] that a state may be pluralist in one of two ways: it may have more than one nation or autochthonous people (such as the Scots, Welsh and Irish in the United Kingdom and the American Indians in North America); or it may have one or more groups of 'allochthonous' people (such as the Turks in Germany and the Greeks in Australia). I shall argue shortly, however, that these two categories do not exhaust the possibilities and that it is important to acknowledge at least one further way in which a state may be pluralist: it may have one or more groups of citizens who choose to identify themselves in terms of a distinctive cultural characteristic, such as religion, rather than according to their nationality or land of origin. The Muslims, for example, are a significant cultural minority in most Western countries; as a group, they contain both immigrant families and autochthonous converts, and they typically draw their primary identity not from their place of origin but from their religious commitments. Let us look more closely now at each of these three categories in turn.

Autochthonous Minorities

The cultural aspirations of national minorities and aboriginal peoples normally involve the desire to preserve their distinct cultural identity and to prevent it from becoming submerged in the culture of the majority. We need first to distinguish such *cultural* aspirations from the *political* experiences of national minorities and aboriginal people. If the latter perceive a sustained inequality of treatment politically by a state that favours the majority nation, then two political consequences are possible. Where the minority group occupies a distinct territory, it may follow the path of secession and seek to establish an independent state, as with the Kurds in Iraq and Iran. And where the minority group does not occupy a distinct territory but is intermingled with the majority there is the possibility of long-term violent conflict, as in Northern Ireland, Israel, Lebanon and Cyprus.

The difficulty of sustaining a group's distinct *cultural* identity, on the other hand, involves different issues. The danger to the minority culture might arise not from a failure on the part of the state to treat the members of the minority group on equal terms with all other citizens, but precisely as a result of such equal treatment. If all the citizens of a state are equally free to work and settle in any part of the state, then over time a territory associated with a particular cultural minority may be settled by other citizens and the territory's distinct cultural identity may not survive. Maintaining the cultural integrity of a minority group within a particular territory may in such circumstances be achieved only by restricting the freedom of choice (in this case to settle freely within the state) of the majority. This could be effected either by the secession of the particular territory from the state, so that effectively a new nation-state is created; or by restricting the freedom of other citizens of the state to settle permanently or change the original character of the territory. The former is exemplified by the demands of Quebecois for secession from Canada,[6] the latter by the demands of Canadian Indians for special rights to ensure their cultural survival[7] and by the struggles of the tribal peoples of the Narmada Valley in India against the construction of a dam which would inundate the forests in and by which they live.[8]

What is at issue in this desire for special status is the belief that a minority's right to cultural survival should sometimes take priority over some of the rights that a liberal democratic state usually guarantees to all its citizens. Is this belief a justifiable one? 'Liberalism 1' responds in the negative; it is, to use Taylor's phrase, 'inhospitable to difference'[9] because it insists on applying the rights of all citizens equally, without exception or differentiation, and because it is suspicious of collective goals.[10] 'Liberalism 2', on the other hand, is 'willing to weigh the importance of certain forms of uniform treatment against the importance of cultural survival, and opt sometimes in favour of the latter.'[11] On this view, cultural membership is a primary good, an essential factor to take into account in judgements about the good life. Kymlicka[12] provides what may be seen as a bridge between the two versions of liberalism when he argues that the protection of a cultural community can justifiably be defended as a primary good on the grounds that it provides a necessary context for choice for its members, but that the goal of protecting the given *character* of any cultural community would conflict with liberal ideals. While this move offers some justification of the claims of autochthonous minorities for special treatment, however, it does nothing, as we shall shortly see, to advance the cause of religious minorities, since the goal of the latter is precisely to protect the character of their cultural communities.

Allochthonous Minorities

This section is concerned with the cultural aspirations of people with cultural or ethnic roots outside the territory of the state in which they have citizenship. We need again to distinguish the difficulties they face in sustaining their *cultural* identity from any difficulties that may be experienced in attaining full citizenship in the *political* community. I shall not be dealing at all with the political problems of guest workers, temporary residents and refugees who have not gained the equal rights of permanent citizens in their country of residence, but only with the cultural problems of full citizens who do not share the nationality or cultural identity of the majority. Such people's identity is often described in hyphenated form, as in Italian-Australian, Black-British or African-American, where the second element refers to their citizenship and the first to the cultural minority to which they belong.

There are two main kinds of difficulty facing allochthonous cultural minorities. The first is a failure on the part of the majority cultural group or of longer-established cultural groups to treat the members of minority groups on equal terms. This may take the form either of an unwillingness to change existing structures in the light of new circumstances of cultural pluralism, or of an explicit or implicit expectation of assimilation. The second is an overt or hidden sense of cultural superiority on the part of autochthonous cultural groups, leading to various forms of prejudice, racism, discrimination, social avoidance and inferior treatment, and also to paternalistic or condescending attitudes, including treating minority cultures as quaint or exotic.

Thus it is not surprising that the desire for equality is a major aspiration of allochthonous cultural minorities. In this they differ significantly from autochthonous minorities. Though they share with the latter the desire for recognition, they differ in two crucial respects: first, the possibility of secession does not come into the question, and secondly, they do not demand (I shall argue) special status in the sense of seeking to preserve their identity by restricting the rights of the majority. I shall argue that none of the demands of allochthonous minorities falls outside the scope of what Taylor calls 'the politics of equal respect'.[13] Even instances which appear to emphasise difference, such as calls for positive discrimination or for elements of African history and culture to be included in the school curriculum, turn out to be grounded in the claim for equal respect. This argument may be illustrated by brief reference to two distinct feminist approaches to equality, which I have elsewhere called the 'egalitarian' and the 'radical feminist'.[14] The egalitarian approach emphasises the need for equal opportunities policies which aim at the eradication of institutional sexism and encourage women to move into male-dominated areas. The radical feminist approach places more emphasis on female solidarity, on the realities of women's experiences and on women gaining recognition for their distinctive qualities, potential and achievements. These two approaches, of course, are not imcompatible or mutually exclusive, but are simply different manifestations of women's striving for equality of respect.

In just the same way, the search by minority cultural groups for equality of respect may take two complementary forms. On the one hand, there is an initial desire to break through the barriers of discrimination and institutional racism by demanding parity with members of other cultural groups. This may best be achieved by full social integration and by the adjustment of social institutions to take account of the cultural pluralism in society. Thus in a system of common schooling it would be necessary to find a way of including minority cultures in a new curriculum for all. On the other hand, equality of respect implies that cultural minorities have just as much right as others to see their own cultural identity as a source of pride, loyalty and personal identity and as something to be celebrated, and that they have the right to ensure that their children are not denied the chance to continue the cultural traditions of the minority. All of this is subject to the condition that supporting the culture of the minority group does not in any way undermine the political community of which the group is part.

This kind of cultural maintenance for a minority group cannot, however, be achieved without some special provision. Let us imagine a hypothetical state with a common school system, in which 96% of the population share broadly the same cultural background and aspirations, and in which there are two distinct ethnic minorities each making up 2% of the total population. If we take for granted the claim made earlier that no curriculum can be culture-free, how should the cultural influences within the curriculum be distributed? An initial response suggests that the proportion of cultural influence should correspond directly to the actual size of the cultural groups involved. However, the percentage of input from the two minority cultures could probably be justifiably increased to 5% each without any arguments for special status being required, because such an increase could be justified simply in terms of the cultural enrichment of the broader society and the fact that these cultures, which are actually part of the overall society, cannot have justice done to them in less. But if the percentage were increased much further, then the likelihood of a backlash from the majority cultural group might also increase. But would a cultural input into the common curriculum of 5% be sufficient to preserve the distinct cultural identity of the children of a minority group? I think not. It would seem that some supplementary provision would be necessary for the minority group, but not for the majority, so that the former could have an equal opportunity to preserve their cultural identity. And if the parents were not able to offer this supplementary provision themselves because of a lack of time, resources or education, then the provision either of supplementary classes within the common school or of supplementary schooling run by the minority community outside normal school hours would seem to be called for. Such differentiated or additional provision would be justified on the basis of equality of respect for minority cultural groups, and it would appear to be the only way in which the kind of hyphenated identity which has already been discussed could be developed or maintained. The use of public funds for such provision would seem no less just than allowing increased public expenditure for the education of differently abled pupils.

All this is allowed for, I believe, within 'Liberalism 1'. Although 'Liberalism 1' is generally associated with the melting-pot and the colour-blind (or difference-blind) approach (which Taylor calls the 'politics of equal dignity'[15]), there is no reason why the protection of the rights of all citizens equally should not extend to their right to a cultural identity (or the 'politics of difference'). On this view, if culture is to be recognised as a primary good at all, it should be recognised as such equally for all (the 'politics of equal respect'). 'Liberalism 2', on the other hand, does not appear to have anything extra to offer allochthonous minorities. In fact, insofar as 'Liberalism 2' recognises the right of a state to promote the distinctive linguistic, cultural or religious heritage of the cultural majority, this may work to the disadvantage of cultural minorities. As we have seen, if a state can justifiably pass a law saying that the language of the majority is the only legal language of the state, it cannot at the same time encourage minorities to preserve their own distinctive linguistic heritage. 'Liberalism 2' may find secession justifiable, that being in effect the creation of a smaller state in which the new cultural majority may again have special rights, and may allow special rights to indigenous peoples in specific territories, but has nothing to offer allochthonous minorities beyond the basic rights of all citizens.

What emerges from this is the unexpected conclusion that 'Liberalism 1' appears to favour allochthonous, and 'Liberalism 2' to favour autochthonous cultural minorities. There are still further complications to explore, however, for we must now turn to a group for whom the terms autochthonous and allochthonous seem inappropriate.

Religious Minorities

The particular minority groups which are the focus of attention here need careful definition. They are similar to autochthonous groups as described so far in that their primary goal is to seek structural change in order to accommodate and preserve their distinctive cultural heritage, but differ in that their culture is not associated with a particular territory within their state of residence, and also in that the preservation of their distinctive culture does not involve significant restrictions being placed on the rights of the majority. They are similar to allochthonous groups as described so far in that many of them have ancestral links with territory outside the state of which they are citizens, but they differ from allochthonous groups in three crucial respects.

First, they are not seeking equity of treatment as such with other cultural groups within the state. Equity could be achieved either by supporting all cultural groups equally or by refusing to support any, as in the American doctrine of the separation of church and state. However, in the eyes of the religious minorities under consideration here, the withholding of public funds from all religious schools, for example, simply disadvantages them all equally in comparison to secularists in their attempts to educate their children in accordance with their own beliefs and values. What such groups want is not parity of treatment with other groups, but the freedom to bring up their own children in line with their own religious commitments.

Secondly, it is their religious commitment, rather than their citizenship, which determines the primary identity of these religious minorities. This distinction may be seen by comparing the hyphenated identity of such groups (for example, British-Muslim) with that of the allochthonous minorities discussed in the last section (for example, African-American). In each case, the element after the hyphen appears to indicate the primary loyalty.

Thirdly, the cultural identity of such groups is not of a form which can be tacked on as an extra component to their citizenship, as supplementary schooling may be tacked on to the experience of the common school for allochthonous children anxious to retain their cultural identity. On the contrary, their religious identity is something which they believe should permeate the whole of life. In terms of the example given earlier, they would find it difficult to accept an education in which for 95% of the time their children were subject to a 'neutral' or secular curriculum while 5% was devoted to their own cultural or religious beliefs and practices. The 95% would be perceived as potentially undermining the faith, and even if the children attended supplementary schools for a substantial amount of time each week, this would not necessarily compensate for the non-religious influence of the common school. At least the children might find themselves pulled in two different directions at once, at a vulnerable or impressionable age. Hence there comes about the desire for separate schools, which their opponents may dismiss as a form of voluntary apartheid, but which their supporters see as the only way to provide the children with a sound education in a secure and stable environment where the beliefs and values of the school are broadly in line with those of the home.

Such groups may find themselves looking with some envy at the 'millet' system of the Ottoman Empire[16] or indeed at the current status of religious communities in Israel. Under the 'millet' system. Orthodox Christians, Armenians and Jews were all recognised as self-governing units or 'millets' (millet meaning literally 'nationality' or 'people united by a common faith'); the legal traditions and practices of each community were respected and they were free to run their internal affairs, worship freely, enjoy limited self-government, obey their own laws and customs and run their own schools.[17] Similarly in present-day Israel every individual belongs to a religious community which has jurisdiction over personal status, including issues to do with marriage, divorce, wills, custody of children and burial; each religious community is free to preserve and cultivate its own culture, both through its own publicly funded separate system of education and through control of its own media. What both the millets[18] and minority religious communities in Israel[19] lack, however, is a strong sense of citizenship or what Ernesto Laclau calls 'political belongingness',[20] and it is this fact which differentiates them from the category of religious minority which is under examination here, as a rather more detailed look at the example of the British Muslims makes clear.

Muslims in Britain make up about 2% of the total population and in addition to being frequent targets for racist behaviour, they find themselves often economically disadvantaged, under-represented in public decision-making processes and correspondingly vulnerable to decisions made by the non-Muslim majority. Social closure[21] appears to have increased group solidarity, and 'British Muslim' is now a widely used way of describing their identity, in preference to earlier imposed identities defined in terms of place of origin, skin colour, status as immigrant or mother tongue. The term suggests that they are seeking recognition both as British citizens and as Muslims. Indeed, many British Muslims believe they have much to offer the broader society, particularly in the area of moral example. However, it is their religion which gives them their distinct identity, and it is their religion rather than other aspects of their cultural heritage which they are most anxious to preserve. Ashraf is at pains to emphasise this point:

> In two or three generations a group of Muslims will emerge who will be British in their use of English, in some of their customs and conventions, even in their love of English literature, but they will be Muslim not only in positive absolute values, but in those values that are completely anti-modernist and anti-secularist.[22]

Their educational aspirations similarly reflect their desire for recognition as both citizens and Muslims. My own research into the Muslim communities in Britain[23] suggests that Muslim parents have two main educational goals for their children:

(i) the preservation, maintenance and transmission of their distinctive beliefs and values, both through direct teaching and through a school ethos informed by these values;

(ii) access to the opportunities offered by a general education, including living as full British citizens without fear of racism or other forms of prejudice, competing in the employment market on an equal footing with non-believers and, more generally, enjoying the benefits of modern scientific and technological progress.

Some Muslims undoubtedly give priority to (ii), and are happy to leave (i) as a private matter to be dealt with at home and in the mosque, particularly if the common school ensures that Muslim children are not required to participate in activities that are against their religious beliefs.[24] Liberals have no quarrel with this group, and indeed they are virtually the same as the allochthonous minorities discussed above. Other Muslims, however, believe that (i) and (ii) must be integrated into a single harmonious education, which means in effect that (ii) must be given a distinct religious flavour and brought into harmony with Muslim beliefs. Their goals could only really be achieved through the establishment of separate publicly funded Muslim schools. The public funding would enable the quality of general education provided by such schools to be brought into line with that of the common school, and would also enable the state to lay down requirements relating to preparing the pupils for citizenship.

Under the heading of 'religious minorities' I am concerned only with this second group, since the first group presents few problems to liberals.

Similar educational goals are found among some sections of the Sikh community in the West, some Hindus, some black Christians, and some orthodox Jews as well as some evangelical Christians.[25] Their desire for separate religious schools is justified partly in familiar communitarian terms — to do with the importance of commitments and cultural identity as a basis for human flourishing—and partly in religious terms: the religion sets a public standard by which people can measure their lives, and the standard lacks significance if it is open to individual interpretation and challenge.

How are liberals to respond to such religious minorities within the context of the democratic state? 'Liberalism 1' provides a clear vision of education: in particular, it rules out (at least in public schools) the uncritical presentation of any concept of the good or of any understanding of the world and human life. Children of all groups need to question their assumptions, to grapple with conflicting world views, to engage in rational debate, and to value diversity of tastes, interests and non-fundamental values. They need to be free to distance themselves from the culture of their parents and to make autonomous decisions about their own commitments, values and life-plans. In this sense, the needs of children do not vary according to the commitments of their parents, and thus education can and should become a common enterprise for the children of all groups in a pluralist society. The provision of public funds for separate schools for religious minorities is thus opposed on the grounds that such schools are unnecessary, socially divisive and educationally harmful. 'Liberalism 1' stands by two main principles which put it at odds with religious minorities: the claim that the legitimate exercise of authority within a group should be subject to the ultimate supremacy of the individual conscience, so that any individual should be free to leave the group and the individual's freedom of choice should not be foreclosed by the activities of the group; and the claim that all beliefs and values should be held in a way which allows them to be modified where the evidence becomes strongly weighted against them.

'Liberalism 2' is less unequivocal in its attitude to groups. It may 'sometimes' allow a society to organise itself round a particular definition of the good life,[26] so long as it grants basic rights to minorities. It may 'sometimes' acknowledge that the importance of cultural survival may legitimately be weighed against 'the importance of certain forms of uniform treatment' without the outcome being automatically tilted towards the latter.[27] But this freedom for cultural groups to defend themselves against the homogenising tendencies of uniform treatment tends to be discussed only with reference to nation-states or to autochthonous minorities.[28] Indeed, as we have already seen, Kymlicka makes it clear that his recognition of the primary good of cultural membership is based on a view of the cultural structure as a context for choice, and he distinguishes the protection of the community as such from the protection of 'a particular preferred vision of what sort of character the community should have'.[29] But this rules out the right of religious minorities, as opposed to national minorities or aboriginal peoples, for example, to preserve their distinct cultural identity, since it is only the former's possession of a 'preferred vision' which makes them a distinct community at all. Their shared identity depends not on a shared cultural heritage—indeed, many religious minorities are multi-ethnic groups—but on a shared framework of fundamental beliefs. If they cannot use education to maintain this shared framework of fundamental beliefs, then their culture is vulnerable either to gradual corrosion as a result of sustained exposure to liberal values or to a more direct assault by liberal social policy. It is not surprising therefore that liberalism may be experienced as oppressive and undermining particular religious traditions. What Western educationalists see as universal liberal values may well be seen by others as secular and reductionist.

In the final section of this paper, I shall consider what sort of moves towards compromise are possible in this apparent principled deadlock, where liberals believe that concessions are being demanded which would be inconsistent with fundamental liberal principles, and the religious minorities believe that liberal values which undermine their distinctive beliefs are being imposed on them. The charge of imposing values on others is not one which many liberals like, though a few have grasped this particular nettle. Raz, for example, with some reluctance tolerates communities whose culture does not support autonomy so long as they are 'viable communities', and hopes for their gradual transformation, but at the same time claims that if the life they offer their young is too impoverished and unrewarding, compulsory assimilation (by force if necessary) may be 'the only humane course'.[30] The earlier Rawls similarly argues that it is only unworthy ways of life that lose out in a just constitutional regime:

> If a conception of the good is unable to endure and gain adherents under institutions of equal freedom and mutual toleration, one must question whether it is a viable conception of the good, and whether its passing is to be regretted.[31]

However, if this represents the hard face of 'Liberalism 1', there is perhaps more hope of compromise, at least in the arena of education, in some of the arguments currently being put forward within 'Liberalism 2'. Commenting on Rawls, Galston points out that the line between ways of life that can flourish in a pluralist context and those whose viability depends on a more hospitable homogeneity 'does not easily divide valuable from worthless, or generous from repressive, conceptions of the good',[32] and he argues that liberal freedom entails the right to live unexamined as well as examined lives.[33] Rawls himself in his more recent writings acknowledges that

> Political good, no matter how important, can never in general outweigh the transcendent values—certain religious, philosophical and moral values—that may possibly come into conflict with it.[34]

Since modern liberal democratic societies are characterised by conflicting conceptions of the good, such matters should be excluded, Rawls proposes, from public discourse. Minority groups should have the maximum freedom consistent with individual freedom of conscience. Thus they may be free to establish their own educational system, or even to withdraw from the modern world in accordance with the injunctions of their religion, so long as they 'acknowledge the principles of the political conception of justice and appreciate its political ideals of person and society'.[35] Finally, there are Taylor's arguments about the presumption of the equal worth of different cultures.[36] So far, I have taken these as an extension of the 'politics of equal respect', leading to the development of a multicultural curriculum and the expansion of the canon of accredited authors in which all children have the right to be culturally literate. However, if we take the presumption of equal worth to its logical conclusion, then this may be taken to indicate that 'all human cultures that have animated whole societies over some considerable stretch of time'[37] have a right to take steps to ensure that own continuation. Such arguments form the starting point for the educational proposals sketched out in the final section.

EDUCATION AND CULTURAL DIFFERENTIATION

The preceding sections have indicated some of the differences between the various cultural minorities which might claim a legitimate interest in using education to preserve and maintain their distinctive cultures, and some of the different liberal responses. In this final section the possibility is explored of a compromise involving the development of a set of educational structures within a liberal democratic state which would generate an equality of dignity and respect for all cultural minorities, including religious ones, enabling them to retain their specific identity and preserve this across the generations, while at the same time allowing them to participate fully as citizens and developing the qualities necessary to make this possible.

The argument in this section involves the claim that liberalism has a cultural as well as a political dimension, and that although the distinction between these is often blurred, they need to be carefully distinguished if cultural dominance within education is to be avoided. Cultural liberalism manifests itself in two ways: first, as a natural extension of political liberalism, and secondly, in the very claim that is often made to cultural neutrality. Political liberalism inevitably overflows into the cultural domain, even where the state does not formally align itself with a nation or with the culture of the majority. For example, there are enormous advantages if a state has a common language which all citizens can use when participating in democratic activities. But the identification of one language as the official language of the state has cultural implications both for the privileged majority who speak it as their mother tongue, and for the cultural minorities with a different mother tongue, who are correspondingly disadvantaged. The search for a substantial set of shared values in a liberal society (on which, for example, to construct a common educational system) is also likely to move beyond the political and encroach on the cultural domain.[38] Secondly, the claim to be culturally neutral or to be a meeting ground for all cultures, which is sometimes made on behalf of liberalism, is itself a cultural stance. For example, liberalism is hospitable to a wide diversity of sexual lifestyles, but is less hospitable to any cultural group wishing to exert a high level of control over the sexuality of its members. Cultural liberalism is perhaps best understood as a framework of conditions within which a number of different cultures might thrive, particularly those which emphasise autonomy and individuality, but which is inhospitable to other cultures, for example, to those which emphasise group interests at the expense of individual freedom.

The distinction between political and cultural liberalism parallels the distinction between the political and the cultural community with which this paper began. If this distinction is accepted, it opens the way for the suggestion that while political liberalism provides the foundation for citizenship education for all the children within a democratic state, cultural liberalism must take its place alongside other cultural ways of life, whose members have an equal moral right to make provision for children's primary cultural development. All the children in a democratic state will grow up to be citizens of that state and will therefore all equally need to learn about the principles of democracy and about the privileges and responsibilities of citizenship. That part of the curriculum can be common for all children. However, not all children in a democratic state will grow up to be members of the same cultural community. If it is true that education cannot be culture-free, then to provide a common education for all children regardless of religion, ethnicity, nationality or mother tongue is likely to tip the scales in favour of some cultural communities and ways of life and against others. Such inequality of respect could be avoided by allowing all cultural communities the right to set up their own schools which would offer common provision with regard to citizenship education, but distinctive cultural education. Schools with a liberal cultural perspective would thus exist alongside a wide variety of denominational schools and schools for pupils of different mother tongues, national origins or other cultural affiliations. All schools would receive public funding, and parents would be able to choose freely among the diversity of schools.[39]

The system under consideration thus involves two key elements: education for democratic citizenship (which is common across all schools), and education for specific cultural attachment (which is different in different schools). To those I would add a third element, which would seem vital for multicultural societies: education for cross-cultural understanding. Each of these elements gives rise to a number of important and complex questions, and further questions are raised by the relationship of the elements to each other in a unified curriculum.

Education for democratic citizenship is an education in those political beliefs and values on which the very existence of a liberal state is based. These values include the recognition of all citizens as equal in respect of fundamental rights and freedoms, the rejection of racism, prejudice and discrimination as an affront to individual identity, and the duty of all citizens to support and uphold institutions that embody a shared conception of justice and the rule of law. As Rawls points out, a strong sense of citizenship is needed to sustain the political virtues of 'reasonableness and fairness, a spirit of compromise and a readiness to meet others halfway'.[40] Education for citizenship thus potentially involves much more than an unreflective initiation into the existing political structures of the state. It may include reflection on principles and values and the critical appraisal of prevailing political structures in the light of these values, as well as encouraging political involvement and participation and developing a sense of obligations and responsibilities to the wider political community. In McLaughlin's terms, therefore, the kind of education for citizenship under discussion here is not limited to a 'minimalist kind of interpretation'.[41] However, since modern liberal democracies are characterised by conflicting conceptions of the good, it is important that education for citizenship should not be seen as promoting any particular cultural conception of the good. Each cultural group must be free to pursue its own conception of the good within a framework of justice and equal respect. The freedom guaranteed to citizens by political liberalism includes the freedom to pursue non-liberal cultural goals.[42] Education for citizenship would simply exclude cultural issues from its agenda and focus solely on political matters,[43] though there remains the danger, as Rawls is aware,[44] that initiating children into 'political liberalism' will predispose them to accept 'a comprehensive liberal conception'.

Education for a specific cultural attachment would be what differentiated the schools within a state and would therefore be one important consideration by which parents made their choice of school. It would be justified on three grounds: (a) a recognition that citizens may have 'affections, devotions and loyalties that they believe they . . . should not stand apart from and objectively evaluate from the standpoint of their purely rational good';[45] (b) the presumption of the equal worth of different cultures, as expounded by Taylor;[46] and (c) the belief that children need a secure and stable environment, at least in their formative years, where the cultural values of the school are broadly in line with those of the home.[47] Schools providing an education in what I have called cultural liberalism would therefore be competing with a variety of other schools offering education based on more specific national, religious, linguistic or other cultural values. Cultural groups might sometimes form alliances in order to provide a viable school (as already happens on a very limited scale in England with joint Catholic and Anglican schools). The concept of education for a specific cultural attachment raises several important questions: would any cultural groups be barred from establishing their own schools? Could a school have a democratic ethos (as required by education for citizenship) and a specific cultural ethos at the same time? Would prejudice be reinforced or an unhealthy rivalry or animosity develop between schools with different cultural attachments? Would the loyalties engendered by the school tend towards divisiveness rather than social integration? Although I cannot debate these questions here, I will indicate possible approaches to them. With regard to the first question, there would undoubtedly be a debate between those who wished to restrict the right to establish schools to 'cultures that have provided the horizon of meaning to large numbers of human beings . . . over a long period of time[48] and those who wished to extend the right to any group whose fundamental beliefs and values were not in conflict with the political values underpinning democratic citizenship. With regard to the second question, it might be argued that schools have a duty to help pupils to learn to balance their civic and cultural commitments. With regard to the third and fourth questions, rivalry and divisiveness would be less likely to thrive in a state which showed an equality of respect towards diverse cultural groups, and suspicion and resentment between groups would be further diminished by education for cross-cultural understanding.

Education for cross-cultural understanding (which could be expected to include a variety of pedagogical approaches, not just formal teaching) would have an important contribution to make in a multicultural society to the development of tolerance and respect and the ability to live alongside groups with different cultural values. It is in fact closely related to education for democratic citizenship, though different groups might interpret education for cross-cultural understanding in different ways: liberals might see it as a precondition to autonomy, so that while children are not *encouraged* to leave their own community, they are at least aware of alternatives; at the other extreme, Muslims may see it as a fulfilment of the Qur'anic injunction to 'know one another'.[49] On the other hand, all groups might see it as a way of encouraging gradual change and development within the cultural community as a result of interaction with others. The identity of Muslims in the West, for example, is undoubtedly influenced by contact with the surrounding cultures, but may nonetheless remain true to core Islamic values.[50]

I have argued throughout this paper that cultural membership is an important part of individual identity which an education system should not ignore, and indeed cultural communities normally provide the context in which children are initiated into moral practices. Cultural membership has perhaps been undervalued in classical liberal theory, but there is a danger that the pendulum might swing too far in the other direction. Too strong an emphasis on national, cultural or religious identity may lead, as Hall warns, to the adoption of 'closed versions of culture or community' and 'the refusal to engage with the difficult problems that arise from trying to live with difference'.[51] I have therefore argued in this final section that education for a specific cultural attachment must be balanced by education for democratic citizenship to counteract its divisive tendencies and that education for cross-cultural understanding will contribute further to the development of toleration and respect within an integrated and genuinely pluralist society.

ACKNOWLEDGEMENT

I would like to thank Terry McLaughlin for his helpful comments on an earlier draft of this paper.

NOTES AND REFERENCES

1. Regarding nationality, see Tamir, Y. (1993) *Liberal Nationalism* (Princeton, Princeton University Press) and Miller, D. (1993) In defence of nationality, *Journal of Applied Philosophy*, 10, 1, pp. 3–16. Regarding race, see Banton, M. (1983) *Racial and Ethnic Competition* (Cambridge, Cambridge University Press) and Sarup, M. (1991) *Education and the Ideologies of Racism* (Stoke-on-Trent, Trentham Books).
2. Walzer, M. (1992) Comment, in: C. Taylor, *Multiculturalism and 'The Politics of Recognition'* (Princeton, Princeton University Press), p. 99.
3. Smolicz, J. J. (1993) Nation, state and ethnic minorities from a Euro-Muslim perspective, *Muslim Education Quarterly*, 11, 1, pp. 17–18, 22.
4. Walzer, M. (1992), p. 99.
5. Cf. Smolicz, J. J. (1993).
6. Cf. Nielsen, K. (1993) Secession: the case of Quebec, *Journal of Applied Philosophy*, 10, 1, pp. 29–43.
7. Cf. Kymlicka, W. (1989) *Liberalism, Community and Culture* (Oxford, Clarendon Press), pp. 142ff.
8. Cf. Jayal, N. G. (1993) Ethnic diversity and the nation state, *Journal of Applied Philosophy*, 10, 2, pp. 147–153.
9. Taylor, C. (1992) *Multiculturalism and 'The Politics of Recognition'* (Princeton, Princeton University Press), p. 60.

10. Cf. Halstead, J. M. (1988) *Education, Justice and Cultural Diversity: an examination of the Honeyford affair, 1984–85.* (Lewes, Falmer Press), pp. 210–219.
11. Taylor, C. (1992), p. 61.
12. Kymlicka, W. (1989), Ch. 8.
13. Taylor, C. (1992).
14. Halstead, J. M. (1991) Radical feminism, Islam and the single-sex school debate, *Gender and Education,* 3, 3, pp. 263–278.
15. Taylor, C. (1992).
16. Cf. Modood, T. (1990) *Muslims, Race and Equality in Britain: some post-Rushdie affair reflections* (Birmingham, Centre for the Study of Islam and Christian–Muslim Relations), p. 9.
17. Kymlicka, W. (1992) Two models of pluralism and tolerance, *Analyse und Kritik,* 13, pp. 33–35.
18. Cf. Hourani, A. (1969) Race and related ideas in the Middle East, in: M. M. Tumin (Ed.) *Comparative Perspectives on Race Relations* (Boston, Little, Brown and Company), p. 164.
19. Cf. Smooha, S. (1990) Minority status in an ethnic democracy: the status of the Arab minority in Israel, *Ethnic and Racial Studies,* 13, 3, pp. 389–413.
20. Cf. Hall, S. (1992) Our mongrel selves, *New Statesman and Society,* Supplement, 19 June, p. 6.
21. Cf.Weber, M. (1968) *Economy and Society* (Eds. G. Roth and C. Wittick) (New York, Bedminster Press), p. 342.
22. Ashraf, S. A. (1986) Foreword to J. M. Halstead, *The Case for Muslim Voluntary-Aided Schools: some philosophical reflections* (Cambridge, Islamic Academy), p. vi.
23. Halstead, J. M. (1986) *The Case for Muslim Voluntary-Aided Schools: some philosophical reflections* (Cambridge, Islamic Academy).
24. Cf. Halstead, J. M. (1988), ch. 8.
25. Cf. Walford, G. (1994) Weak choice, strong choice and the new Christian schools, in J. M. Halstead (Ed.) *Parental Choice and Education: principles, policy and practice* (London, Kogan Page).
26. Taylor, C. (1992), p. 59.
27. *Ibid.,* p. 61.
28. Cf. Walzer, M. (1992), p. 100.
29. Kymlicka, W. (1989), pp. 167–168.
30. Raz, J. (1986) *The Morality of Freedom* (Oxford, Clarendon Press), pp. 423–424.
31. Rawls, J. (1975) Fairness to goodness, *Philosophical Review,* 84, p. 549.
32. Galston, W. (1991) *Liberal Purposes: goods, virtues and diversity in the liberal state* (Cambridge, Cambridge University Press), p. 275. Cf. also Rawls' reply: Rawls, J. (1993) *Political Liberalism* (New York, Columbia University Press), p. 198, footnote 33.
33. Galston, W. (1989) Civic education in the liberal state, in: N. L. Rosenblum (Ed.) *Liberalism and the Moral Life* (Cambridge, MA, Harvard University Press), p. 100.
34. Rawls, J. (1988) The priority of right and ideas of the good, *Philosophy and Public Affairs,* 17, 4, p. 275.
35. Rawls, J. (1993), p. 200.
36. Taylor, C. (1992), pp. 64–73.
37. *Ibid.,* p. 66.
38. McLaughlin, T. H. (1992) Citizenship, diversity and education: a philosophical perspective, *Journal of Moral Education,* 21, 3, pp. 240ff.
39. Cf. Hargreaves, D. (1994) *The Mosaic of Learning: schools and teachers for the next century* (London, Demos).
40. Rawls, J. (1993), p. 163.
41. McLaughlin, T. H. (1992), p. 238.
42. Cf. Galston, W. (1989), p. 100.
43. Cf. Rawls, J. (1993), Lecture IV.
44. *Ibid.,* pp. 199–200.
45. Rawls, J. (1985) Justice as fairness: political not metaphysical, *Philosophy and Public Affairs,* 14, 3, p. 241.
46. Taylor, C. (1992).
47. Cf. McLaughlin, T. H. (1984) Parental rights and the religious upbringing of children, *Journal of Philosophy of Education,* 18, 1, pp. 78ff.
48. Taylor, C. (1992), p. 72.
49. Watt, W. M. (1979) *What is Islam?* (London, Longman), p. 233.
50. Cf. Halstead, J. M. (1994) Between two cultures? Muslim children in a Western liberal society, *Children and Society,* 8, 4, pp. 312–26.
51. Hall, S. (1992), p. 8.

Learning from Mistakes: Resources of Tolerance in the Jewish Tradition

MENACHEM LORBERBAUM

Many contemporary discussions of religious education focus upon obligations which liberals may have towards religious education.[1] These discussions inevitably draw upon the virtue of tolerance and the value of pluralism to make room for non-liberal traditions within the educational framework of the liberal state, even though these traditions often do not share liberal values. Indeed, some of the religious traditions that we might be obliged to tolerate in contemporary liberal societies may even be devoted to furthering values at odds with basic liberal concerns such as autonomy and equality.

The problem of religious schooling, however, is more than a mere borderline case testing the rational coherence of liberal theory. The question of religious schooling today reveals a problem reaching to the foundations of many modern polities where we cannot simply assume an homogenous civil-society. The individualistic conception of liberalism removes children from their specific familial and communal setting, viewing them (from the state's eye) as unmediated citizens. It is no wonder, then, that the state's institutions come into conflict with the social setting of the students, especially when the parents or community have a strong interest in their own culture's conservation and perpetuation. These tensions are intensified in the case of religious schooling because modern liberalism has its historical roots in the overthrowing of a predecessor culture that was manifestly religious.

But do religious schools have an interest in responding to the liberal agenda? Do they have an interest in furthering values such as tolerance and pluralism?

Part of the answer depends upon the degree to which religious communities view themselves as participating in the larger enterprise of the polity. There are often immigrant communities in the United States, in Britain and elsewhere whose members view their new country as a haven and place of refuge but not as the framework in which they would like to exercise their rights as citizens or develop their personal identity. Such a community has an interest in preserving cordial relations with its host but no more. The core of its spiritual life lies in an 'old' world or in a newly created reservation in the new one. This is true of some Jewish orthodox communities in the United States and even, paradoxically perhaps, in Israel too.[2] It is also true of certain Muslim communities in the United Kingdom.[3] The continuing existence of segregated communities is also a matter of state policy. If liberal education is imposed by the state through common schooling and strict control of the curriculum, these communities will either have to find economic resources for private schooling or cease to exist.

Alternatively, religious communities may seek ways to accommodate liberal values while retaining their religious identity. Such a project can further the chances of broadening the common moral ground within the polity, thus contributing to the circumstances of pluralism where social homogeneity cannot be assumed.

A central concept in such an effort is that of tolerance. The particular role of tolerance comes out when contrasted to both liberalism and pluralism. The virtue of tolerance can play an important ancillary role but cannot, properly speaking, be a primary concept of liberalism. Liberalism typically makes stronger claims than a theory based on virtue would allow. Liberalism is a theory of justice predicated upon rights. The claims made by any individual based on her rights result in an obligation imposed on her interlocutor. She is not expecting tolerance, she demands obligation. For example, the right to freedom of speech does not merely demand of the listener to tolerate but rather places an obligation upon him not to silence the speaker. Liberal rights can be well complemented by tolerance but liberalism cannot be constituted by tolerance. As a cardinal virtue, tolerance is therefore typically pre-liberal or post-liberal. It features in the political theories of thinkers such as Spinoza[4] and Locke who precede liberal societies.[5] Yet it does not play a central doctrinal role among philosophers such as Mill or Rawls. Tolerance re-emerges today in a consciously multicultural society whose thinkers do not assume a morally homogenous society.[6]

Tolerance is also distinct from pluralism. Pluralism is the doctrine that holds 'that human goals are many, not all of them commensurable, and in perpetual rivalry with one another'.[7] Tolerance in pre-liberal political theories was a virtue construed to fit monist rather than pluralist conceptions of the good. What makes tolerance a powerful virtue in such contexts is the claim that even when one knows the truth, one can be limited in the political consequences that result therefrom. On this understanding, toleration is exercised towards an interlocutor whom we hold to be wrong or in error. We tolerate the other's mistake.[8] A theory of tolerance will therefore include not only a political argument about the limits of legitimate coercion, but also an epistemology that makes possible the identification of error and an acknowledgement of its place in a given culture.

Ultimately, the project of accommodating liberal values can be forwarded only when religiously committed individuals perceive secular liberalism as a challenge rather than as a threat. The liberal challenge to authoritarian religious anthropology is that of human beings affirming their freedom and assuming responsibility for their destinies. Such a stance of human self-perception inevitably affects one's standing before God, and affects also the authoritative social structures that draw their legitimacy from the divine-human relationship.[9] But focusing upon tolerance has a specific contribution in that it disconnects the claim to truth from immediate consequential coercive action. It aims precisely at the least liberal religious elements, weakening the connection between belief and aggression.

For reasons of both validity and effectiveness, arguments for toleration must come from within the tradition. In one sense, traditions provide a range of acceptable and authoritative argumentation and discourse, but also 'traditions, when vital, embody continuities of conflict'.[10] Within the Jewish tradition, the Talmud supplies both. It is a wide-ranging source of argumentation; indeed, its literary structure is of a rhetoric that celebrates argumentation. And this rhetorical quality is closely linked to a midrashic hermeneutic that has a very open-ended notion of textuality.[11]

In this article, I will outline a model of educating for tolerance for a Judaism that acknowledges rabbinic authority. It focuses on one of the components of a theory of tolerance, namely the epistemology of mistakes. The model is based upon an analysis of a particular talmudic discussion.[12] Needless to say, the talmudic sages were not precursors of modern liberalism. This fact, however, does not preclude the pedagogical adaptation of resources in this tradition for developing new models for religious education.

Developing an argument from within necessitates a shift in normative discourse: from the liberal discourse of rights, pluralism, and autonomy to rabbinic argumentation. I will first introduce the particular background of the text. Cultural translation is not an easy task but it is a necessary capacity for life in a multicultural society — certainly for the effort of promoting tolerance between different cultures.

The talmudic sages define the characteristics of a *talmid hakham*, a student of the wise, in contra-distinction to the biblical roles of prophet and priest.[13] In contrast to the prophet who claims a direct revelation of divine will, the sages are equipped with an hermeneutic capable of deciphering a revealed text whose canonisation effectively signifies the end of direct revelation. Rabbinic Judaism is a text-centred Judaism that assumes a democratisation of the text, and that in turn sets it apart from the priestly religion too.[14] Contrary to priestly claims to privilege of rank based on an intimacy with God afforded by the temple, the sage offers the text of equal access as a basis for intimacy and religious knowledge.

The intertwining of epistemology, hermeneutics and social structure which sets rabbinic Judaism apart from its biblical predecessors finds unique expression in tractate *Horayot*, i.e. (court) rulings, of the Mishnah. *Horayot* deals with mistaken instructions issued by a court and mistaken transgressions committed by other public functionaries, and the sacrificial sin-offerings thereby incurred.[15] It occasions a talmudic discussion of mistakes and of the connection between knowledge and responsibility. The questions explored by the talmudic discussion are: what constitutes a mistake? and what obligation is incurred when a subordinate realises the authority is mistaken?

TEXTUAL ANALYSIS

The first mishnah of *Horayot* states:

> If the court [mistakenly] ruled to transgress any one of the *mitzvot* (commandments) mentioned in the Torah, and an individual proceeded to act in error accordingly: whether they acted and he acted along with them, or they acted and he followed them, or they did not act and only he acted — he is exempt

[from a sin-offering], because he depended on the court . . . This is the rule: whoever depends on himself is liable, and whoever depends on the court is exempt.[16]

This mishnah distinguishes between an individual acting on his own and an individual guided by the court. The former 'depends' upon himself, the latter upon the court. Thus, 'if the court ruled to transgress any one of the *mitzvot* mentioned in the Torah, and an individual proceeded to act in error accordingly', he is exempt from a sin-offering. Because he followed the court's instruction and thereby acted according to the court's (mistaken) knowledge, he cannot be considered to have sinned wilfully. He is thus dependent upon the court.

It is important to note that expiatory sacrificial rituals apply only to cases of unwitting transgression; a wilful transgression is punished. But the case at hand is not a usual case of acting unwittingly because the individual intentionally committed the sinful act. However, the mishnah seems to regard this case too as one of unwitting action ('and an individual proceeded to act in error [*shogeg*] accordingly'), and lays the responsibility on the court.[17]

The mishnah is interested here in an individual's transgression only in so far as it is a result of his dependence upon the court's ruling and not a result of his own ignorance. It is this dependency which exempts him from responsibility.[18] The mishnah stresses that the dependence is that of knowledge and not of action: 'whether they acted and he acted along with them, or they acted and he followed them, or they did not act and only he acted — he is exempt [from a sin-offering].' His own exemption is not dependent upon their action but upon their claim to knowledge.

What is a legitimate claim of dependency? The Mishnah and Talmud develop the notion of dependency by considering the manner in which it might be severed. This can be done in one of two ways: if the court cannot claim true knowledge; in other words, if its decision is not even a mistake; or if the individual is sufficiently knowledgeable to render him independent; in other words, if he should have known better.

The first point is addressed by the Mishnah later on in the chapter:

If the court gave a decision uprooting an entire body [of law] . . . if they said there is no [law] of idolatry in the Torah, they [the court] are exempt. (1:3)

Uprooting an entire body of law cannot be a mistake. This point is reminiscent of Wittgenstein's argument that 'there is a difference between a mistake for which, as it were, a place is prepared in the game, and a complete irregularity that happens as an exception'.[19] The difference between an irregularity and a mistake is that a mistake has grounds:

If my friend were to imagine one day that he had been living for a long time past in such and such place, etc. etc., I shall not call this a *mistake*, but rather a mental disturbance, perhaps a transient one . . . a *mistake* doesn't only have a cause, it has a ground . . . when someone makes a mistake, this can be fitted into what he knows aright. (*On Certainty*, paras. 71 and 74)

Irregularity is typified by lack of a framework into which we can fit 'what he knows aright'. The difference between irregularity and ignorance is that the ignorant individual cannot be mistaken because he simply does not know. Similarly in our case: uprooting an entire body of law defies the very rules of the game, so to speak. If it is due to ignorance, it is less than a mistake. Thus the mishnah concludes that if the court

> gave a decision that partly annulled and partly sustained [a body of law] they are liable [for the congregation sin-offering]. How so? If they said — 'idolatry does exist [as a body of law] in the Torah but if one bows down [to an idol] he is exempt' — they are liable. For scripture says: 'and the matter escapes [the notice of the congregation]' — a 'matter' not an entire body.

It is possible to deliberate over whether bowing is a mode of worship, but it is impossible to deliberate about the very prohibition of idolatry.[20]

The second point is addressed in the last clause of mishnah 1:1 which reads:

> If the court ruled and one of its members, or a student worthy of ruling, knew they had erred, but proceeded to act accordingly: whether they acted and he acted along with them, or they acted and he followed them, or they did not act and only he acted — he is liable [for a sin-offering], because he did not depend on the court.
>
> This is the rule: whoever depends on himself is liable, and whoever depends on the court is exempt.

Court members, or mature students, are not considered dependants of the court because they should have known better.

The Talmud moves the discussion forward. It wants to understand the student's considerations in following an erring court when he knows them to be wrong:

> 'Or a student worthy of ruling.' Like whom? Rava said: Like Simeon ben 'Azzai and Simeon ben Zoma.

Simeon ben 'Azzai and Simeon ben Zoma are prominent sages who are not ordained, and are described elsewhere as 'discussants before the sages' (BT Sanhedrin 17b).[21] But identifying them does not tell us much about the nature of their error. Moreover, ben 'Azzai and ben Zoma were of such a learned reputation that the fact that they were not ordained does not make a difference to the basic matter at hand:

> Said Abaye to him: Is this a case of inadvertent transgression?!

People of their stature should know better and therefore cannot be considered unwitting transgressors and cannot be expiated by a sin-offering.

Rava answers that the mishnah refers to a student who knew that the particular act sanctioned by the court was forbidden,

> but he erred in [assuming] it a *mitzvah* to adhere to the words of the sages.

This mistake is one worthy (perhaps typical?) of the learned. It is a mistaken submission to authority.

The Jerusalem Talmud goes a step further. It too begins its discussion by raising the question of the nature of the student's deliberation:

> Rabbi Imi said in the name of Rabbi Simeon ben Lakish: The mishnah refers to a case like Simeon ben 'Azzai sitting before them.
>
> What is the case? If he is knowledgeable of the whole Torah and ignorant of that particular matter—he is not Simeon ben 'Azzai, and if he knows that particular matter but is ignorant of the whole Torah he is like Simeon ben 'Azzai for that particular matter?
>
> Rather the case is of one who is knowledgeable of the whole Torah and of that particular matter, but he errs in thinking that the Torah said: 'follow them, follow them'.

But the Jerusalem Talmud is not satisfied with the solution:

> But if he errs in thinking that the Torah said 'follow them, follow them', he is not a Simeon ben 'Azzai?!

This again raises the question of whether this is a case of inadvertent transgression. Shouldn't the student have known better than to follow the court in error? In order to answer the question, the Talmud must find a basis for construing the deliberation whether one ought to follow the opinions of the wise even if one is convinced that they err as a deliberation worthy even of a Simeon ben 'Azzai.

This is addressed by the barraita:[22]

> Can it be the case that if they [i.e. the court] say to you that right is left and left is right you should listen to them? Scripture therefore teaches us 'to the right or to the left' [Deut. 17:11]—that they say to you right is right and left is left.

The Talmud's answer consists of two stages: first, the inner midrash quoted in the barraita; second, using this midrash to answer the question of a worthy mistake.

The barraita provides a midrashic interpretation of a verse in Deuteronomy that concerns the authority of the High Court:

> If there arise a matter too hard for thee in judgement . . . then shalt thou arise, and go up to the place where the Lord thy God shall choose; and thou shalt come to the . . . judge that shall be in those days and inquire; and they shall tell thee the sentence of judgement; and thou shalt do according to the sentence . . . and thou shalt observe to do according to all that they inform thee . . . thou shalt not deviate from the sentence which they shall tell thee to the right or to the left. (17:8–11)

According to this midrash, 'right' and 'left' restrict the scope of the court's authority. The court's authority is binding only if 'they say to you right is right and left is left'.

The Talmud quotes this barraita because by raising the student's doubt — 'Can it be the case that if they say to you that right is left and left is right, you should listen to them?' — it implies that the student's mistake was based on a valid assumption. It is only on the basis of a novel midrashic interpretation that the barraita deduces that the student must trust his own judgment as to right and left. Indeed, there are tannaitic sources which clearly advocate the opposite:

> 'To the right or to the left'. Even if they show you to your own eyes that right is left and left right — listen to them. (*Sifre Deuteronomy* 154)

According to this midrash, 'right' and 'left' illustrate the extent of the court's authority. One is to obey their ruling 'even if they show you to your own eyes that right is left and left right'.[23]

The question of the limits of obedience raises a legitimate doubt and therefore gives grounds for a mistake worthy of the learned.

EDUCATIONAL MODEL

The talmudic discussion pointed to two kinds of mistakes. There are mistakes made by an authority in interpreting normative texts. These mistakes are characterised by grounds and limits. There are also mistakes committed by subordinates to this authority. This is the mistake of undue submission to an erring authority.

The main point of the talmudic discussion is the recognition that there is such a thing as mistaken submission. The Talmud thus creates space for conscience as a limit to legitimate authority. The discussion assumes authoritative interpretation, but it also assumes that this interpretation can be wrong. The judge of error is the individual student sitting before his teachers who is responsible for his choice and cannot excuse himself as dependent upon them.

An educational model which would take its cue from this talmudic discussion would feature a number of elements:

1. Institutions of authoritative interpretation.
2. The possibility of mistaken interpretation. In other words, the authority to interpret does not preclude the possibility of error.
3. A roughly prescribed field of argumentation. These are the rules of the language game. They make possible a distinction between error and ignorance.
4. A recognition of the value of individual integrity of judgement.

The model is characterised by its attempt to balance an adherence to authority with an obligation to retain personal integrity.

This balance is buttressed by two features of the talmudic tradition which are illustrated by the discussion quoted above. The first feature is the discursive style. The Talmud is premised upon learning as a value. Talmud means study, and study begins when someone is engaged by the wisdom of earlier generations. The activity of Talmud is dialogical: an encounter with a tradition of texts different from myself that make normative claims upon me. But it also assumes that engaging in their study includes the ability to argue one's point by questioning the coherence and, at times, the validity of this textual tradition.[24]

The second feature is that of midrashic hermeneutics. Midrash assumes the authority of the text it interprets but lends it a pliability that generates meanings instead of just constraining them. For example, the metaphors of right and left can be read rigidly and one-dimensionally to stress that one should not wander from the straight path directed by the court. However, both the midrashic readings quoted above treat these metaphors instead as indicators of the scope of judicial authority. For these midrashim the metaphors have implications that touch upon the central issues of the verse. Midrash is a method of teasing out meaning from these individual words while listening closely to the text.

The capacity to generate meanings in the present context is not primarily meant to satisfy aesthetic criteria of literature.[25] Midrash is a judicial as well as a literary tool. A text-centred tradition must develop rich methods of encountering foundational texts if these texts are to continue to carry the burden of normative guidance for successive generations. It is not the mere listening but the engagement in interpretation that sustains the vitality of discourse as a tradition.

The scope of legitimate toleration produced by this model depends upon a number of factors:

1. What are the limits of legitimate deliberation posed by this talmudic discussion? It is this aspect of theories of tolerance that most troubles liberals because at this point the difference between tolerating a deviant opinion or an error and celebrating freedom is clearly perceived. As a parallel, recall Locke's argument for toleration that leaves atheists out: 'those that by their atheism undermine and destroy all religion, can have no pretence of religion whereupon to challenge the privilege of a tolerance'.[26]
2. Who is to be considered knowledgeable? The Mishnah speaks of 'a student worthy of ruling'. The inadequacy of this criterion is implied by the Jerusalem Talmud's remark that 'if he knows that particular matter but is ignorant of the whole Torah, he is like Simeon ben 'Azzai for that particular matter'. This question is linked to the next one.
3. What are legitimate sources for argumentation? Knowlege of right and left is accessible to all. Is this knowledge metaphorical for knowledge gained by reason and moral sensibility apart from inherited wisdom?[27]

Yet these questions do not diminish the recognition accorded to the notion of a mistake in this talmudic discussion. Committed liberals cannot be satisfied with less than freedom but they need not neglect the importance of tolerance in non-liberal societies. An educational model predicated on this talmudic discussion could help further the resources for tolerance, first by cultivating an awareness of the liability to mistake against the pretence to absolute knowledge and, second, by stressing the role of individual conscience. A student can err 'in [assuming] it a *mitzvah* to adhere to the words of the sages'.

APPENDIX

Tractate *Horayot* can be viewed as the rabbinic restatement of the biblical portion of sin-offerings in Leviticus 4. A comparison of the structures of these two texts points directly to the rabbinic 'revaluation of (biblical, *sic*) values'. The biblical chapter deals with cases 'when a person unwittingly incurs guilt in regard to any of the Lord's commandments' (Lev. 4:2). The particular sin-offerings for expiation of the transgression are determined by the sinner's rank:

> The anointed (high) priest (verses 3–12) → The whole congregation of Israel (13–21) → Chieftain (*nasi*, 22–26) → A person from the people of the country (27–35).

The hierarchy expressed in the structure of these laws views the high priest as the pinnacle of the congregation. He precedes the congregation as a whole, and he is viewed as their representative. The high priest and the congregation bring the same sacrificial offering, and it is he who performs the same rituals within the sanctuary in both cases. Next in line is the chieftain who brings a less prestigious offering—a goat, not a bullock—and it is an ordinary priest who performs the necessary rituals. The people of Israel are hence viewed primarily as a congregation, not a polity, and it is the high priest who most successfully represents them, not the political figure head of the *nasi*. Last in this list comes the ordinary individual who is characterised by the range of offerings he can bring according to his (meagre) means.

Tractate *Horayot* deals primarily with public officers. Its structure is as follows:

> The court (chapter 1) → The anointed priest (2:1, 3:1–3) → King (the rabbinic understanding of *nasi*, 3:3).[28]

The Mishnah's hierarchy clearly puts the rabbinic court at the pinnacle—even though the court is not one of the options mentioned in the original biblical chapter which is the basis for the Mishnah's discussion!

This position is based on the following midrashic interpretation. The opening verse of the sin of the congregation reads:

> If it is the whole community of [*'adat*] Israel that has erred and the matter escapes the notice of the congregation [*kahal*], so that they do any of the things which by the Lord's commandment ought not to be done . . . (4:13)

The midrashic interpretation centres on the change of noun describing the sinning agent: *'edah*, community, and *kahal*, congregation. The use of the synonymous *'edah* invites a comparison to the word's other occurrences in the Torah:

'adat yisrael [the community of Israel]: Might scripture be referring to the whole of the community? Scripture therefore teaches us by saying *'edah*, here and saying *'edah* below (Numbers 35:24: 'the *'edah* shall judge between the slayer and the blood-avenger'). Just as the *'edah* referred to below is a court, so too here it is a court.[29]

The rabbis interpreted the case of 'the sin of the congregation' as a case of a mistaken ruling issued by a court. The audacity of this interpretation becomes clear when we consider the fact that the court thus assumes the role of the representative of the people as a whole and the priests are a subordinate role to them.

The novel role attributed to the sage is summarised in the last mishnah of the tractate:

A priest precedes a Levite [to be saved in a life-threatening situation], a Levite an Israelite, an Israelite a bastard [*mamzer*], a bastard a bondsman, a bondsman a proselyte, and a proselyte a freed slave. This applies only when they are [otherwise] equal; but if a bastard is learned in the Law [*talmid hakham*] and a High Priest is ignorant of the Law, the Bastard that is learned in the Law precedes the High Priest that is ignorant of the Law. (3:8)

The study of Torah is a new source of status in this society. It is an acquired status in that its achievement depends upon the intellectual activity of the individual, and it is thus valued beyond the inherited status of priesthood. But although the rabbis introduce a new set of values with the potential for far-reaching social consequences, they stop short of using it as a revolutionary lever for transforming the basic hierocratic structure of their Jewish society. The rabbis subordinate the priesthood but leave it as a privileged class. This is apparent in our mishnah which accepts the priestly hierarchy when all things are equal. It features again in the Mishnah's laws of permitted marriages (Kiddushin 4:1).[30]

NOTES AND REFERENCES

1. See e.g., T. H. McLaughlin, The ethics of separate schools, *Ethics, Ethnicity and Education*, edited by M. Leicester and M. Taylor (London 1992), pp. 114–136; J. M. Halstead and A. Khan-Cheema, Muslims and worship in the maintained school, *Westminster Studies in Education*, vol. 10 (1987), pp. 21–36.
2. A. Ravitsky, *Messianism, Zionism and Jewish Religious Radicalism* (forthcoming, Chicago, 1995), chapter 4; G. Cromer, Withdrawal and conquest: two aspects of the Haredi response to modernity, in: *Jewish Fundamentalism in Comparative Perspective*, edited by L. J. Silberstein (New York, 1993), pp. 164–180. For an example in the U.S., see I. Z. Rubin, *Satmar: An Island in the City* (Chicago, 1972). On pluralism in Israel see G. J. Jacobsohn, *Apple of Gold: Constitutionalism in Israel and the United States* (Princeton, 1993), pp. 18–54.
3. Cf. Halstead and Khan-Cheema, *op. cit.*, and M. Halstead, Radical feminism, Islam and the single-sex school debate, *Gender and Education*, vol. 3 (1991), pp. 263–278; Ethical dimensions of controversial events in multicultural education, in: *Ethics, Ethnicity and Education*, edited by M. Leicester and M. Taylor (London, 1992), pp. 39–56.
4. *Theological-Political Treatise*, Chapter 20.
5. In the 'Letter concerning Toleration' as distinct from the *Second Treatise Concerning Government*. Locke scholars have noted that contrary to William Popple's declaration in the introduction to his translation of the Letter that 'absolute liberty, just and true liberty, equal and impartial liberty, is the thing we stand in need of', Locke in the Letter argued for toleration and not liberty. See J. W. Gough, The development of

Locke's belief in toleration, and M. Cranston, John Locke and the case for toleration, in *John Locke, A Letter Concerning Toleration in Focus*, edited by J. Horton and S. Mendus (London, 1991), pp. 71, 85. Regarding the degree of continuity between Locke's different works see also P. Nicholson's article, John Locke's later letters on toleration, in the same collection, pp. 163–187.

6. 'As Britain has developed into a multi-cultural and multi-racial society, so the need to define the scope of and limits of racial and religious toleration has grown', *Aspects of Toleration*, edited by J. Horton and S. Mendus (London, 1985), introduction p. 7. This introduction, however, conflates toleration and freedom. In a later article, Locke: toleration, morality and rationality, Horton and Mendus 1991, pp. 147–162 (note 5 above), Susan Mendus stresses both the difference of perspective we have from Locke and also the contemporary relevance of his arguments.

7. I. Berlin, Two concepts of liberty, *Four Essays on Liberty* (Oxford, 1969), p. 171.

8. We also speak of tolerating difference. But although difference is often a psychological and social cause of persecution, it is not in inself a moral ground for persecution. Mistakes, however, *prima facie* require intervention. Tolerating error is an argument for limiting what might seem to be a valid moral ground for intervention.

9. See D. Hartman, *A Living Covenant* (New York, 1985), pp. 1–18, and *Conflicting Visions* (New York, 1990), Part 3; M. Sokol, Personal autonomy and religious authority, in: *Rabbinic Authority and Personal Autonomy*, ed. M. Sokol (New Jersey, 1992), pp. 169–216.

10. A. MacIntyre, *After Virtue* (Notre Dame, IN: 1984), p. 222. The special social circumstances of religious communities in liberal society intensify the need for the social criticism from within described by M. Walzer in *Interpretation and Social Criticism* (Cambridge, 1987).

11. See D. W. Halivni, *Midrash, Mishnah and Gemara* (Cambridge, MA, 1986), and M. Halbertal, *People of the Book: Canon, Meaning and Authority* (forthcoming, Cambridge, MA, 1995).

12. Babylonian Talmud (BT) Horayot 2a–2b, and Jerusalem Talmud (JT) Horayot 45d. A full theory of tolerance would include a discussion of legitimate coercion, BT Baba Batra 47b–48a, and of the limits of rabbinic authority, BT Sanhedrin 86b–89a.

13. See BT Baba Batra 12a–12b, Yoma 71b. Post-war ultra-orthodoxy has been characterised by a concept of rabbinic knowledge with prophetic undertones: see L. Kaplan, Daas Torah: a modern conception of rabbinic authority, *Rabbinic Authority and Personal Autonomy*, pp. 1–60.

14. For the sake of brevity I am using fairly broad brush strokes. Rabbinic culture is nurtured by the inner tensions of law, history and wisdom inherited from the bible. There are also important differences within the priestly tradition, and midrash is of course rooted in biblical literature itself: See M. Fishbane, *Biblical Interpretation in Ancient Israel* (Oxford, 1985).

15. See the appendix for a short analysis of the structure of the tractate and its relation to the transformative character of rabbinic Judaism.

16. Unless otherwise indicated, translations of rabbinic material have been prepared by Noam Zohar and Menachem Lorberbaum for a forthcoming work by Michael Walzer, Noam Zohar and Menachem Lorberbaum entitled *The Jewish Political Tradition*.

17. The Talmud noticed this point and raises the following discussion: 'Let it be taught "and he acted in accordance with their ruling"; what need was there for "through error"?–Raba replied: [The addition of] "through error" [was meant] to include [the following case]. If the court ruled that suet (forbidden fat) was permitted [to be eaten], and a person mistook suet for [permitted] fat and ate it, he is exonerated . . . Others read: . . . he is liable' (2a) *Babylonian Talmud*, Nezikin vol. 4, Horayoth, translated by I. W. Slotki (London, 1935).

18. For the limits of individual claims of ignorance see BT Shabbat 67b ff.

19. *On Certainty*, edited by G. E. M. Anscombe and G. H. von Wright and translated by D. Paul and G. E. M. Anscombe (Oxford, 1974), 647.

20. See Mishnah Sanhedrin 7:6. The Talmud there (62b) discusses the case of an individual who assumes idolatry to be permitted; cf. BT Makkot 7b.

21. They are described as esoteric adepts in BT Haggigah 14b.

22. Literally, external, i.e. a tannaitic teaching not included in the Mishnah.

23. Important medieval commentaries on this issue are Judah Halevi, *The Kuzari* 3:35–38; Maimonides, *Mishnah Torah*, Laws concerning Rebels, Chapter 1; Nahmanides, *Commentary to the Torah*, Deuteronomy 17:11. There are a number of suggestions for reconciling the two midrashim quoted above in Kaplan, *op. cit.*, pp. 29–33.

24. See BT Shabbat 30b.

25. Cf. Umberto Eco's definition of the novel as 'a machine for generating interpretations', *Reflections on the Name of the Rose* (London, 1985), p. 2.

26. Letter concerning Toleration, p. 47. Locke's argument in this sentence is different from the preceding sentence where he argues about what he takes to be the political dangers of atheism.

27. It is in this context that the questions of medieval Jewish philosophy become particularly interesting. Philosophy begins by questioning the very enterprise of revelatory law: see Saadya, *The Book of Beliefs and Opinions*, translated by S. Rosenblatt, (New Haven, 1976), introduction, p. 31.

28. According to rabbinic interpretation the *nasi* 'is the King, for it is written, "And doeth any one of all the things which the Lord his God hath commanded [not to be done] — a Ruler that has above him none save the Lord his God' (*Horayot* 3:3), *The Mishnah*, trans. by H. Danby (Oxford, 1983).

29. *Sifra on Leviticus*, ed. L. Finkelstein (New York: JTS, 1983), vol. 2, p. 141.

30. These laws are rooted in Ezra's attempt to turn the returning exiles into a people of the temple: see Ezra, chapter 2, and chapters 8–10. This is a clear illustration of how rabbinic Judaism remains deeply intertwined in the priestly heritage.

Educational Rights in Multicultural Democracies

COLIN WRINGE

EDUCATION AND TRADITIONAL COMMUNITIES

Certain outcomes which in liberal democratic societies are regarded as undoubted components of the individual's right to education run, all too frequently, into confrontation with traditional groups who perceive them not only as misguided and spiritually dangerous to their members but as threatening to their group's identity and even its continued existence. The Amish, or Plain People, rejecting all wider learning beyond that necessary for the continuance of their simple way of life,[1] would be an obvious and hackneyed example. Few traditional groups, however, are happy with forms of religious education other than the uncritical transmission of their own beliefs. The teaching of Science may be seen as conflicting with, or at least tending to undermine, traditional cosmologies. Current notions of Health Education, particularly those that seek to empower individuals to define and work to meet their own health needs[2] may provoke a measure of hostility, while introducing the young to a study of literature and the creative and performing arts may seem to support values which some communities regard as frankly scandalous. Certain general educational aims inseparable from the concept of a liberal democracy are equally at odds with approved ways of life and thought in many traditional communities. Such aims will include that of promoting equality of opportunity, irrespective of race, religion and gender and of developing individuals' personal autonomy and ability to control and manage their own lives. In the past these have been the tacit goals of many enlightened educators. Increasingly they are recognised as being among the explicit curricular aims of democratic educational systems.[3]

Such conflicts of value will be a source of discomfort to many democrats who wish to seem tolerant to traditional groups living in their countries, particularly when these are minorities which are in certain respects underprivileged. It will, however, be my purpose to argue that their anguish is to no avail for ultimately there is no way we can avoid confronting the fact that many traditional cultural groups are profoundly anti-democratic in those very central beliefs which hold them together and give their ways of life coherence and being. It will be otiose to give examples of groups prepared to shed blood for such propositions as that:

— morality and religious belief are not matters of autonomous judgement or individual reflection but of authoritative pronouncement;

— parents may prevent their children from marrying and raising a family with someone of another faith, particularly if that means sharing the way of life of that other person;

— one's own religious beliefs, values and form of social hierarchy have been revealed as the only true ones, and those who believe, let alone teach, otherwise are in error; error has no rights and may be summarily punished;

— the adherents of certain religious beliefs are properly privileged above others, while even adult women and children are subject to arbitrary paternal power and authority.

Towards a monocultural society embodying such beliefs, the democrat's attitude would be unhesitatingly critical. Indeed, it was precisely the existence of such regimes that gave rise to the democratic movements of the European Englightenment, while communities that form minorities in states aspiring to be multicultural may themselves be culturally and ethnically linked to monocultural states elsewhere which do little to encourage toleration of other cultures within their boundaries, and are roundly condemned by democrats in consequence.

The conflict between individual rights and the claims of traditional communities to regulate the conduct and access to knowledge of their members raises well-known questions about the relationship of the state both to individuals and to groups within it. For liberals, as we know, the individual is prior to the state. The state exists to provide a secure framework within which individuals may pursue their own particular goals. What those individuals do or believe privately is no business of the state's provided they do not interfere with other individuals or threaten the state's good order. As a way of reconciling democracy and intercultural tolerance one might be tempted to take an analogous position with regard to relations between the state and cultural groups: that what cultural groups get up to privately is their own business, so long as they keep their hands off other groups and do not threaten the state's good order.

Clearly this is unsatisfactory. States may differ from communities in important respects but states and communities resemble each other in that both consist of distinct and separate individuals. If individuals may not be sacrificed to the state, it is difficult to see how their important interests may be set aside against their will for the good, cohesion or continued survival of whatever other groups they may happen to be born into. Such important interests will necessarily include those benefits which flow from a broad enabling education. These may be of a material kind, allowing one to escape a life of drudgery, ill-health or fear of violence and abuse. Alternatively they may lie in the value which some attach to the opportunity of choosing among a range of alternative ways of life, even if the values underlying these alternatives must themselves have been generated by communities of which one is, or has been, a member.[4] Many individuals having such a possibility of choice may freely and deliberately choose to continue to adhere to the beliefs, values and ways of life current in their community of origin. This will be unsurprising when — as is of course often the case — these beliefs, values and ways of life are indeed valuable and recognisable as such by an educated and rational person. Wherever the interests of an individual may lie, however, to be committed to democracy is to be committed to protecting these interests against that of the group, even when that group is a cultural entity which, as a democrat, one wishes to respect and, within the parameters of democracy, try to preserve.

For democrats are also committed to ensuring that individuals do not suffer discrimination or disadvantage as a result of their membership of particular communities and to ensuring that customs and practices which are neither publicly disruptive nor unjust or harmful to individuals are not interfered with or vilified. Democrats may also be committed to lending positive support to ways of life that are valued by those citizens engaged in them, and which might otherwise be threatened by modern conditions. The assumption must however be that power relations within those communities are compatible with the demands of democratic values or that membership is at least voluntary in the sense that all are not only free to leave, but have access to the knowledge and skills that would enable them to choose whether or not to do so.

COMMUNITY MEMBERSHIP, NATIONAL POLITICS AND THE ROLE OF EDUCATION

We may be tempted to entertain the naive picture of a multicultural society as one in which a secular government deals even-handedly with the various cultural groups that compose it and in which politics and cultural identity are seen as separate. Muslims, Jews, Catholics, Jehovah's Witnesses and Secularists may vote Republican or Democrat, Labour or Conservative, Centre Left or Centre Right without reference to their cultural group. In such a context, multiculturalism raises few political problems. The state merely has to monitor systematic bias in public appointments and the distribution of benefits and services, intervene with the support of all responsible citizens to put down outbreaks of youthful intergroup hooliganism, ensure sensitive and flexible attitudes in its school teachers and curriculum builders and generally encourage the cultural enrichment of society as a whole from the colourful variety of inputs offered by its constituent groups.

This picture bears little resemblance to reality in many countries, where ethnicity may be of desperate political importance and those born into the wrong group face a lifetime of economic deprivation, political disenfranchisement, official harassment, and worse. The dominant group protects its domination, not necessarily in the name of some odious notion of cultural superiority — though this may be present — but simply out of common interest with kith and kin. One has no sense of identity or sympathy with other groups who are thought of as aliens. For their part, the dominated may see themselves as outcasts who, even if not in active rebellion, have no commitment to the interests of the mainstream society.

In such a situation, majoritarian democracy (one person, one vote) serves only to perpetuate injustice against minorities. The only morally acceptable outcomes are partition, which may be impossible where there is any degree of territorial intermingling, group representation which risks producing its own injustices and, despite probable opposition from traditional groups, a sustained educational effort to supplement group values and loyalties with others of a wider kind. If our country is called Illyria, then at least in our public life, we must sometimes place justice to our Illyrian fellow-country-persons before our community loyalty as Greek Orthodox, Catholics, Jews, Muslims, or whatever. Unless we do this, there can be no talk of our being a multicultural society. Indeed we are not a society at all but a collection of separate, mutually hostile societies, jockeying for position, waiting for the moment when we shall have the advantage and may legislate our rivals into subjection or be rid of them altogether.

What are required are values which all can be expected to share, but not all such are equally desirable. Aggressive patriotism, for example, simply removes the problem of conflict to the state's external boundaries. A commitment to democracy, on the other hand, is at least a reputable starter, capable of engaging the idealism of its supporters and having built-in tendencies towards reconciliation, mutual respect, dialogue and the relief of hardship and oppression.

Whatever resistance they may encounter, educational goals based on openness, enquiry and rationality, not to mention models of Religious Education which promote mutual understanding and the recognition of common ground and Health Education which encourages individuals to identify and articulate their own needs, are valid, not only in terms of their ostensibly intended outcomes but as means of promoting dispositions and values favourable to democracy, such as a readiness to dialogue, tolerance and independence. Though good democrats are bound to be conciliatory, such activities may well provoke hostility from those who see community separatism or intercommunal strife as supportive of their own position within the group, or their political aspirations outside it. For as long as this can be avoided, however, these activities, along with more overt attempts to promote democratic and other supra-communal values, serve to build up a sense of common citizenship which entails looking for justice, education, protection and the means of material and emotional support outside the community framework and, perhaps more importantly, helping to make these things available for others in a way that is sensitive to cultural affiliation insofar, but only insofar, as this does not inhibit individuals' access to what is their democratic entitlement as citizens.

Such a process would aim at developing a sense of national identity in public life, capable of counteracting that other traditional cultural identity which divides us from our fellow citizens, causing us to see them not as such but as enemies and rivals for power and resources. The boundaries between the public and the private, the secular and the communal, the spheres of democratic justice and provision and traditional ways of life are, of course, essentially contestable and some groups may actually deny the existence of such boundaries, holding that all things belong to God and none to Caesar. In the nature of the case, it is not possible to avoid this problem and efforts to do so are wasted. Education in a democracy particularly in areas related to religion, health practices and power relations between different categories of individuals, especially within the family, is bound to be perceived as an incursion into what has previously been regarded as a private or communal domain. If, however, social cohesion and the well-being of all citizens are proper concerns of a democratic society, such interventions must be regarded not merely as legitimate but as obligatory, and the vigour or lack of it with which they are pursued will be a matter not of right but of strategy.

DEMOCRATIC JUSTICE AND COMMUNITARIAN ETHICS

Against such a recommendation we must take account of ethical theorising[5] which tends to disparage such democratic values as equality, autonomy, justice and, above all, individual rights, treating these as no more than emotive preferences within particular styles of rhetoric and having no more, in fact rather less, validity than the values of individual traditional communities. Principal among the arguments given in favour of this view are that:

1. Our individual identity is not to be understood except in terms of the role expectations accorded us by our community and its particular structure. If, for example, we have rights, these are the rights traditionally associated with that role, and the same applies to our duties.[6]
2. Values and practices have no other justification than their contribution to the preservation of the community in which they are practised and of its way of life. A demand for justice would be no more than a demand to be treated in conformity with those values and a demand for equality, if it were appropriate at all, would simply be a demand for the same treatment as others occupying the same role as ourselves. Justice, on such a view, will consist in treating the occupants of similar roles equally, but sees no problem in treating the occupants of different roles differently.

To take this ethical stance seriously, and it is certainly taken seriously by some, would be disastrous for any attempt at intercultural accommodation, not to mention any kind of education for democracy. It is the very practice of seeing oneself, and more especially those outside one's community, not as individuals suffering pain, deprivation, uncertainty, humiliation, the frustration of aspirations and so on, but as the occupants of roles ascribed to them by the mythologies and belief systems of one's community that is at the root of much intercultural strife. One comes all too easily to see oneself as a defender of the true faith, meting out just punishment to heretics and infidels and their descendants, or as the true inheritors of the land keeping usurping interlopers in their place.

Analogous cultural stereotyping may desensitise us to hardship and suffering within as well as between communities. Sufferings which are seen as a traditional or 'natural' part of 'a woman's lot' or the treatment customarily accorded to the halt, the lame or the feeble-minded in our community will not move us to action. Why should they if equality, justice and rights in their democratic connotation are mere trendy rhetoric and, in any case, not traditionally the concern of people like ourselves?

Seen in this light, educators who tell our children that the beliefs of other groups may have something to be said for them, encourage our womenfolk or our labourers to forget their place and become assertive about their rights or health needs or foment discord by uniting deviant outcasts to demand the same treatment and respect as others, must seem either weak-minded and feeble in defending the traditional way of life, or threatening agents of propaganda and subversion. The fear is perfectly justified since it is to be hoped that society will not be unchanged by the democratic education of its children.

I will not here attempt to take on the big guns of Communitarian Ethics beyond drawing attention to what seem to be two palpable flaws in their position.

First, the fundamentally relativist assumption underlying the communitarians' ethical position, namely that values, obligations and rights are not universal, but can only be created by the practices of communities, seems untenable. It is no fact of purely limited or local human experience that individuals are radically separate from each other in their experience of pleasure and pain or frustration and have each but one life to enjoy. Nor is it possible to find any convincing reason for regarding one individual's suffering, well-being or fulfilment as more important than another's. Those who regard their own aspirations as more important and seek to defend a way of life and system of values which support their view may, at best, be guilty of self-deception and, at worst, of complacent self-interest.

At a personal level, sensitive democrats will at least wish to take seriously humane and thoughtful representatives of many established cultural communities which claim divine or scriptural authority for views and practices which are incompatible with democracy. Philosophically, however, it is difficult to distinguish such claims from those of others who use what is essentially the same argument in justification of systems of value and belief which require sex with young children, the surrender of personal property to the community, the isolation of young converts from their families or a readiness on the part of individuals to defend the cult leader at the cost of their own lives or, under certain circumstances,[7] take their own lives and those of their children rather than surrender themselves to the civil authority.

Secondly, the communitarian view is mistaken in treating communities as something clearly defined, separate and unchanging. An individual may mentally inhabit the traditional community of his forebears and suppose that his wife and children will carry on the tradition of simplicity, obedience and separateness from other communities that he himself has followed. These latter, however, in the flux and movement of the modern world — and it is precisely this that the defenders of traditional communities seek to prevent — may, through contacts at school, in the women's group or wherever, have come to see themselves as part of a larger and quite different community. Even the longest-established traditional community will once have been in a state of emergence and differentiation from some other community, but Communitarian Ethics often gives us little positive help in deciding to which community individuals truly belong, though each community may have its own formal or informal rules, claiming them for itself.

In its possessive sense, we 'belong' to no group. We are our own men and women with our own lives to lead. Possibly an individual may be of a disposition to remain within or return to the way of life in which he or she happens to have been born. To the democrat, however, there can be no moral justification for demanding that unwilling individuals should simply accept pre-existing hierarchies or value systems which presume to prescribe whom they shall serve, what knowledge they shall have access to and whom they may turn to in satisfying their needs. To be a democrat is to be committed to the view that if these things are to be prescribed at all it can only be on the basis of rules which could be negotiated between equals, on equal terms. Any other conception of democracy deprives it of its very justification.[8] In an earlier age, the origins of rationality and the liberal values of justice and democracy have been ascribed[9] to just such a contact between different groups with conflicting values and institutions as now obliges us to confront the question of legitimate relations within a multicultural society.

It may be thought that the arguments I have presented are somewhat unfriendly towards traditional communities. My aim has not, however, been to advocate an aggressive melting-pot approach to democratic education producing a uniform generation of identical young democrats whose only link with their cultural heritage is through dim memories of their grandparents' old-fashioned ways. Nothing but sensitivity and respect is merited by those aspects of traditional community life which assert values which do not license injustice or physical or psychological cruelty. Indeed, if it is true that individuals cannot in principle choose their own destinies, values and ways of life unless these notions have first been conceptualised within established communities with their firm assertion of specific systems of belief and conduct, then such systems of belief and conduct should later be capable of modification in the light of the individual's widening experience and developing powers of rational criticism.

A democrat might go further and accept that some people and situations are impossible to change for the better and that attempts to do so may do more harm than good. In such a situation it might even be right to tolerate limited injustices for one generation, but this must be the limit of the democrat's tolerance, for lives blighted by unnecessary suffering, oppression, isolation or restricted opportunity cannot be relived under better conditions. Given, furthermore, the horrific nature of our modern instruments of strife, we cannot afford to live otherwise than at peace with each other, and peace based on oppression either of groups or of categories of people within groups is necessarily fragile. In the end people will simply rebel at whatever cost rather than put up with it.

The democrat's readiness to subvert certain community beliefs and practices may seem arrogant and brash, but not all those who insist upon the value of supposed community traditions are necessarily disinterested or sincere. Those who do so in defence of their own advantageous position within those groups or in support of political ambitions in the wider society may be perverting or desecrating those traditions more truly than those who attempt to soften group differences in the interests of reconciliation, humanity and respect for others, which must be fundamental to any value system worthy of the name.

ACKNOWLEDGEMENT

The original version of this paper, read at the International Conference on Education for Democracy in a Multicultural Society in Jerusalem in June 1993, formed part of a symposium entitled 'Religion, Health Education and Education for Democracy in a Multicultural Society'. The other symposiasts were Denis Bates and Gaye Heathcote of Manchester Metropolitan University and Martha Ramon of the Israel National Self-Help Clearing House. The central ideas in this paper were developed in extensive discussions prior to the conference with Dr Heathcote and Dr Bates, to whom the present writer is greatly indebted.

REFERENCES

1. see Houlgate, L. D. (1979) Children, paternalism and rights to liberty, in: O. O'Neill and W. Ruddick (eds), *Having Children: philosophical and legal reflections on parenthood* (New York, Oxford University Press, 1979).
2. see Heathcote, G. (1994) Health in the community: contradictions posed by an 'empowerment' model of health promotion, *Journal of Applied Community Studies* 6 (1994), pp. 31–35.
3. see, for example, National Curriculum Council, *The Whole Curriculum* (London, National Curriculum Council, 1990).
4. see Kymlicka, W., *Liberalism, Community and Culture* (Oxford, Oxford University Press, 1989), pp. 95–96.
5. by such eminent writers as Alasdair MacIntyre (*After Virtue*, London, Duckworth, 1981), Richard Rorty (Postmodernist bourgeois liberalism, in R. Hollinger, ed., *Hermeneutics and Praxis*, Notre Dame, IN, University of Notre Dame Press, 1985), Michael Sandel (*Liberalism and the Limits of Justice*, Cambridge, Cambridge University Press, 1982) and Charles Taylor, Philosophical Papers 2: philosophy and the human sciences, Cambridge, Cambridge University Press, 1985).
6. see especially MacIntyre, *op cit.*, pp. 64–68.
7. see *The Times*, 23 July 1993, p. 3.
8. see Wringe, C., *Democracy, Schooling and Political Education* (London, Allen & Unwin, 1984).
9. e.g. by Sabine, G. H., *A History of Political Thought* (London, Harrap, 1963).

Selective Index